SPICE

Over 90 Flavourful Paleo & AIP (

I am not a doctor and no part of this publication should be used as a substitute for professional medical advice. This book is a collection of recipes designed to inspire those already following the paleo and autoimmune protocol diets and is for entertainment purposes only. The author is not responsible for any adverse effects that arise from the use of information in this book. I have researched the information that applies to the paleo and autoimmune protocol lifestyle and diet but this information can change over time. Please follow the advice of your health practitioner.

Your health is important. Always check with a doctor or other qualified medical professional if you are concerned about your health or before making any changes to your diet.

Dedication

This book was written for all of you who have decided to improve your health using diet and lifestyle.

It can be tough at times, but it's well worth it.

Listen to your doctor, eat more vegetables, laugh every chance you get, worry less and get plenty of sleep. All while enjoying the odd curry and naan bread.

Wishing you all the best, from me to you.

With love.

Table of Contents

About Me

I love curries.

I spent my late teenage years and early 20s ordering spicy, hot food that was so fiery it would make me feel light headed and dizzy. It didn't matter if it was Thai, Indian or Chinese, the hotter and greasier, the better. And all washed down with beer, wine and maybe a boozy coffee after dessert.

I'd always order as many side dishes as I could fit on the table, too. Chewy, doughy naan breads, crisp prawn crackers, fried chilli-flecked chicken legs, crunchy poppadoms, samosas... I just loved it all. Ginger, chilli, lemongrass and garlic. Spices like cumin, coriander and paprika.

All good.

Until I started the autoimmune protocol diet to help heal my psoriasis patches.

Then I found out I had to give up nightshades - at least potentially for a month or two - along with most of the spices I loved. And naan bread. It was really tough.

The thing is, although I loved all of this hot, greasy, spicy food, I found out later that it hadn't loved me back quite as much. I had digestion problems - fluctuating stomach acid and mysterious IBS that no one knew the cause of, but it was being controlled each day with medication. My psoriasis patches were dry, itchy, burning patches of red, scaly skin that dotted my back, stomach, knees, elbows and face. It covered my entire scalp, where it was at its worst. Hairdressers would cringe as they parted my hair. One doctor I went to see visibly winced. A little girl once asked me why I had sugar in my hair. It wasn't exactly confidence-boosting stuff. So it was no wonder then, that I was on anti-depressants as well.

I spent most of my adult life itchy, in constant pain, unable to leave the house and severely depressed.

Two years on and things are very different. My digestion has never been better. And all but one patch of psoriasis has disappeared completely from my skin. And as a bonus, I no longer feel depressed and withdrawn.

I followed the strict elimination phase of AIP before reintroducing foods and found out that dairy seemed to bring back the heartburn and stomach ache I'd suffered with for so long. Chillies and tomatoes gave me indigestion pains, often so bad I couldn't sleep at night. And sugar, alcohol and nuts seemed to aggravate my psoriasis. It's worth noting that this was personal to me - many people uncover different triggers after an elimination diet like this.

Nowadays I eat a mostly paleo diet with limited coffee and nightshade and seed spices. I generally avoid alcohol and dairy (I can tolerate small amounts of butter and white wine) and nuts, and I watch my sugar intake. My psoriasis is pretty much under control.

But, my goodness, it was tough not eating curry and stir-fries for all that time.

I thought that if I could find a way around the cravings, and develop recipes that were similar to the ones I used to love but were still healthy, healing and fitted with the autoimmune protocol, that it might help others following AIP as well, who also got a Friday night curry craving, like I did.

And so I did.

I set to work experimenting with ingredients; creating curries, stews, soups and stir-fries that reminded me of all those takeaway favourites, as well as fragrant, herb-scattered meals using spices and aromatic foods. I aim to show that even though on AIP you are working with a shortened list of ingredients, you can still cook many of the foods you love without compromising your diet and health. You just need to experiment a little bit along the way, be more adventurous and create brand new spice blends. And in this book, I've done most of that for you.

My blog, *Comfort Bites*, is dedicated to good, healing comfort food no matter what diet or lifestyle you follow. I strongly believe that even if you're on an elimination diet you can still find comforting foods that make you feel good.

I'm so grateful for that day I decided to take my healing into my own hands and stopped relying only on my doctor to heal me. As I looked after myself more and ate well, got enough sleep and reduced my stress, it was like my doctor and I were a team, instead of me just turning up demanding my monthly prescription.

And it was the best decision I ever made.

Good luck with your healing journey.

About SPICE

We all use herbs and spices in our cooking. But how how many of us get stuck in a rut with the flavours we use in our food? It's easy to stick to a few favourites time and time again - a pinch of thyme here, some cinnamon there. I mean, there are so many different kinds, how are we supposed to know when and how to use them?

Herbs and spices are brilliant. They can completely transform a dish. You could sprinkle a stew with parsley and thyme after cooking and it will taste grassy and fragrant. Sprinkle the same stew with mint and coriander instead and you'll end up with a fruity, citrus flavour. A handful of herbs and spices can completely change the flavour of the whole dish.

So how can you use herbs and spices in your cooking? The good news is that there are lots of possible flavour combinations, even if you're on a healing diet that eliminates many spices, like the autoimmune protocol. On AIP, certain spices like nightshades, black pepper and seeds are out in the beginning, at least. Some people find they can reintroduce many of these back into their diets. But even with a limited spice rack, you can still enjoy Thai and Indian-inspired foods, BBQ seasonings and warm, fragrant stews. You just have to be a bit more imaginative, but I aim to show you how you can do this easily with incredible results and have fun at the same time.

With over 90 AIP-compliant, paleo recipes here, you'll soon be making rich, warming curries. Or snuggling up on a Friday night with a home-made, AIP-compliant Chinese meal. Fancy something spicy? There's a horseradish and beetroot dish that's perfect alongside smoked mackerel. Oh, and you want to make sushi? No problem. That can be AIP, too.

As well as flavour, herbs and spices can have herbal and medicinal qualities. Did you know that sage was traditionally thought to be good for the complexion and was used to make ointments for oily skin? Or that in Medieval times, rosemary was thought to aid the circulation? The medicinal qualities of foods such as ginger, turmeric and garlic are being researched and findings suggest that they could provide benefits to our health.

It took me over a year and a half to write this book. I researched lots of different AIP-compliant herbs and spices and tried them out in various dishes - many of these didn't work and so aren't included here. The ones that made it have been tweaked and re-tweaked until I felt that that they had an authentic flavour and passed the test. These are the meals we all enjoy regularly at home, and I hope you will too.

As well as being totally AIP-compliant, all the recipes here are also suitable for paleo diets and are grain, legume, gluten and dairy-free.

I've made this book as user-friendly as possible. The recipes are split into sections: Nibbles and Soups, Main Courses, Sides, and Drinks and Desserts. But at the back I've also included a Recipe Index tailored to type of cuisine - Indian, Thai and Chinese - as well as to dietary requirements (e.g. vegetarian, vegan and low-FODMAP). This way, you can use the indexes to quickly find recipes you'd like to make, depending on what you fancy eating or your personal dietary allowances. You can take this and plan an Indian-style curry night, or a Chinese takeaway night of your own.

And if you have the search function on the device you're reading this on, you can search for certain herbs by typing it in the search box - to reveal information and recipes relevant to that ingredient. There's also the index in the contents page too.

So whether you're craving a noodle soup that you can twirl your fork around - or a rich beef curry that you can dip AIP naan breads into then I hope these recipes will help inspire you.

AIP-Compliant Spices and Aromatics
So which spices can you eat on AIP? At first, it seems as if there's a really long list of ingredients that you need to avoid. So just focus on the ones you can eat. Here's a list of the spices you can use freely, even on the strict phase of the autoimmune protocol.

lemon balm	mace
basil leaves	marjoram
bay leaves	onion powder
chamomile	oregano
chervil	parsley
coriander leaf/cilantro	peppermint
chives	rocket/argula
cinnamon	rosemary
cloves	saffron
curry leaves	sage
dill	salt
fennel bulb	savory
fennel leaf	spearmint
garlic	tarragon
garlic powder	thyme
ginger	truffle/truffle salt

horseradish root	turmeric
kaffir lime leaves	vanilla
lavender	wasabi
lemongrass	watercress

The Spices

Let's have a look at the main spices and other aromatics featured in this book.

Basil leaves

Peppery, fragrant and fruity. Basil leaf is traditionally paired with mozzarella and tomato in a classic Italian 'tricolour' salad, and a few leaves ripped into a tomato sauce (or no-mato sauce) just before serving gives a vibrant freshness and sweetness. It's beautiful with chicken and in home-made pesto sauce and salad dressings. Basil is a key ingredient in my Thai-flavoured curry pastes where it adds richness and sweetness, lifting the flavour of the other ingredients. It's also at home with fruits - strawberries, lime, lemon and raspberries. Basil is a delicate herb, and it's best sprinkled over hot dishes towards the end of cooking. As for storage, basil shouldn't be kept in the fridge, where the low temperatures turn the leaves black and limp. Keep it at room temperature and use it as soon as possible after purchase - a bunch of basil won't keep for long on the worktop or in the cupboard. Dried basil is also available and has a completely different flavour - less fruity but still sweet, and slightly more aniseed-like. You can also buy Thai Basil, which is slightly less fruity in flavour but still sweet. The leaves are a more muted, less vibrant green and they can also be used in Thai curry pastes and dropped into stir-fries.

Balsamic Vinegar

Although balsamic vinegar isn't exactly a spice, it gives a richness to a whole variety of dishes. Trickle a few tablespoons into a beef stew as it cooks and you'll really taste the difference. Balsamic vinegar adds a roundness, a bit like a rich, deep-flavoured red wine - to salad dressings, roasted and grilled meats and marinades. I use it quite often when I need a burst of rich, deep flavour to any dish. It's also good with squash, roasted sweet potatoes and carrots, too.

Bay leaves

Often bought dried, bay leaves are added to stews, where they give a rich, slightly earthy flavour, and they're good thrown in the pan when you're frying fish, too. Instead of being eaten, they're usually taken out and discarded once they've had a chance to infuse their flavour into the dish. Bay leaves are common in French cooking and form part of a typical bouquet garni - a bundle of herbs tied up and left to infuse a dish while it cooks.

Chives

Chives are a member of the allium (onion) family. The long, deep-green tubular blades look a bit like grass, and it has a distinctive mild onion-like taste. Chives are beautiful sprinkled over fish, chicken, pork and most vegetables. I love them snipped into small pieces and beaten into sweet potato mash. Don't be tempted to leave the chives long and cook them - they're quite chewy and not easy to eat this way. For best results snip them into small pieces with scissors or cut them with a sharp knife. If you buy a bunch of chives, these are best kept in the fridge until needed.

Coriander Leaf/ Cilantro

It's often said that you either love coriander leaf or hate it. I love it. It's a bright green leaf with slightly frilly edges and is commonly used in Indian cuisine, to add colour and contrast to a dish, as well as decorate a curry or stew. Coriander leaf gives a fragrant, almost citrussy, lime-like flavour. It's a main component of a good green Thai curry paste and is also good blended up into marinades and dressings. Coriander leaf is another delicate herb, so it will wilt quickly when added to hot food. I love to eat big handfuls of the leaves over an aromatic curry, or over a pulled pork salad. You can store a bunch of coriander in the fridge, but use it as soon as possible - it doesn't have a very long shelf life once cut. Coriander leaves pair well with avocado, lime, lemon, sweet potatoes and carrots. It's worth noting that coriander leaves are AIP-compliant, but the seed (as in ground coriander) isn't.

Cinnamon

A warm spice that you'd immediately think of for flavouring fruit and sweeter dishes, but it's one of the ingredients I use for my Indian style curries, because it adds warmth. You can buy it ground and add a pinch or a spoonful to a recipe, or buy it as a cinnamon stick and leave it to infuse, like when making a chai tea or ice cream. Try a pinch of cinnamon over coconut manna or in whipped coconut cream to add warmth to a dessert. Cinnamon is traditionally paired with apples, but it's also fantastic with pears, berries and oranges, too.

Cloves

You can buy cloves whole or ground. Ground cloves is a dark powder and you only need a small amount to add a warm, autumnal spice to a recipe. Too much and it could overpower the dish. I use a pinch of cloves as one of my base ingredients for an Indian-style curry. Whole cloves are often dropped into a liquid or stew while it cooks - this gives a slightly more muted flavour than just using ground cloves. The warm, wintery tone of cloves complement oranges but also apples and most other fruits. The tiny cloves are also traditionally pressed into gammon or ham before roasting.

Dill

This leafy, aromatic herb has a beautiful aniseed flavour which works perfectly with fish such as salmon, and helps to cut some of the fattiness of the dish. Try adding chopped dill to tuna salads, sardines or mackerel. It's also beautiful with white sweet potatoes and parsnips. When scattering dill over fish dishes, the bright, green feathery leaves give a beautiful contrast to the fish, whether its a soft, pale seabass or a blushing, coral salmon fillet. Dill is often used in pickle recipes and is also popular in Scandinavian cooking, too.

Fennel

Fennel has a similar flavour to dill, only slightly sweeter and more mild. You can eat the feathery fronds as well as the striped, crunchy bulb. Either will give a sweet aniseed flavour. I love fennel with mushrooms, and also the bulb quartered and then roasted with fish such as trout and salmon. I love the crisp edges a fennel bulb has after a few minutes roasting in the oven - a beautiful golden, toasty sweetness.

Garlic

I use garlic in so many of my dishes, and always have a bulb or two on hand in the fridge. The best bit about this pungent bulb is that it's so versatile. Chop it finely or grate it and it has a strong, almost spicy flavour. Thinly sliced, fewer of the oils are released and so the flavour is slightly more mild. And roast a whole bulb, in its papery skin, it in a hot oven for 30-45 minutes (cut the top of the pointy end of the bulb first, and wrap in foil) and the cloves turn soft and paste-like, golden and toffee in colour and quite sweet and aromatic. As well as fresh garlic bulbs, you can buy garlic powder which is good for marinades and seasonings. There's also smoked garlic, which has a soft, mild bonfire flavour to the bulbs. Look out for fermented garlic too, often sold as black garlic. It looks like regular garlic from the outside of the bulb - maybe slightly browner in colour - but when opened, reveals soft, black, sweet cloves that taste almost like treacle or molasses. They can be eaten raw or chopped and used in various dishes.

Ginger

I've come to find ginger such a staple ingredient in my cooking. If I'm feeling a bit under the weather I make a simple ginger tea by infusing a chunky slice in hot water for a few minutes and then sipping it. It really does seem to settle my stomach. It adds an incredible citrussy-spicy flavour to stir-fries and stews, too. Ginger root is pale, golden-silvery and knotty-looking with a yellow coloured flesh. I usually cut off a chunk about the size of my thumb to use in most recipes and I peel it before chopping or grating it finely. Ground ginger is handy for marinades and curries - and although it doesn't have quite the same citrus-freshness and spice that fresh ginger has, it's definitely worth keeping to hand in the kitchen.

Horseradish

One of my favourite spices for adding the kind of heat that clears your airways and tingles on your tongue. Horseradish is from the same family as wasabi and will help clear your sinuses if you have a cold! It's a long, knobbly root that looks a bit like a thick twig or branch from a tree. Once it's peeled, you can see the pearly-white flesh underneath. Grate it and add to dressings, stews or make a traditional-style horseradish sauce that's great with steak or roast beef. As well as beef, horseradish pairs really well with smoked fish, salmon and beetroot. Keep it in the fridge after purchase.

Kaffir Lime Leaves

These leaves of a lime tree are most often bought dried. They do add a mild citrus-flavour to dishes. I love to add a couple to a beef curry or a Thai-style soup or stew, for added flavour. You usually remove them before serving. If you see a recipe that calls for Kaffir lime leaves and don't have any, you can always try adding a little lime peel to the dish instead, for a similar flavour.

Lemongrass

These papery sticks don't look like much, but peel off the outer layers of their covering and they smell incredible. They taste a bit like a cross between lime and lemon and they have a sweet flavour. The lemongrass stalks have a coarse texture though, so you can either trim the stalks and cut them in half, dropping into a soup or stew to let them infuse their flavour, or chop them up and blend using a high-powered blender to make a curry paste. Use lemongrass in Thai style recipes and in desserts to give a gentle, sweet-citrus flavour. Lemongrass is good with fish and seafood, chicken, beef and coconut.

Mace

A pinch of mace adds warmth, and a sprinkling in a burger recipe or pork hash gives it that distinctive sausage flavour that you might be used to. It's another of those spices you need to handle with caution - too much could easily overpower a dish, so use a pinch or two at a time. A good pinch of mace can also balance out the 'liver' flavour in a home-made liver pâté.

Parsley

You can buy two main types of parsley: flat-leaf and curly. The flavour is almost identical, but many feel that the flat-leaf variety looks better in recipes. I use either, with no preference, purely depending on what's available in the shops. Parsley is a main ingredient of chimichurri salsa, and is perfect for every day dressings and marinades. It pairs brilliantly with lemon and other herbs like thyme and coriander. Sprinkle a roughly chopped handful of the leaves over a stew to add colour just before serving. Parsley is also a popular choice for adding to smoothies.

Mint

Mint grows in abundance - where it's planted it often takes over other neighbouring plants. And that's kind of good, because mint is a really versatile herb. Finely chop it and serve with roast or slow-cooked lamb, or sprinkle some of the chopped leaves in a cooling, refreshing raita. It also adds freshness to a mojito-style drink, where the leaves can be added whole to the drink and muddled in the glass until they release their aromatic, sweet scent. Dried mint is available, but I'd always use fresh over dried, because the flavour is so different. Some chefs have started to experiment with mint and fish recipes, claiming that using a very small amount can take away the 'fishiness' of some dishes.

Rosemary

This herb was the symbol of remembrance in Medieval and Tudor England, and it would often be hung up on special occasions like weddings, or made into wreaths and placed at graves. It's a very strong, sweet smelling herb - you'll be able to smell if you're near a rosemary bush in summer. Rosemary is a robust, woody herb, and stands up well to the heat of an oven or grill. Traditionally it's eaten with lamb but is wonderful with roast pork, beef and chicken, too. In my first ebook, *Simple AIP Paleo Comfort Food*, I created a recipe for slow roasted pork belly with rosemary, and it's still one of our favourites. Snip off the stalks and wash them, running your fingers down the spiny leaves so they fall off. Chop them finely before adding to recipes, or, as I did with the pork, strew the pine-like leaves over the meat before roasting.

Rosemary works wonderfully with lemon and other citrus fruits and roasted starchy veggies and is also often added to hot and cold drinks.

Saffron

The world's most expensive herb. These tiny strands are bright amber in colour and come from a crocus flower. As well as brightly stain all dishes a beautiful sunset orange colour, they have an earthy, sweet flavour, too. It's one of the main herbs used in a Spanish Paella and can be used in sweet dishes as well as with citrus fruits, chicken and fish. The strands are either added to the recipe as they are, or left to infuse in a little boiling water before this is poured into the dish. Try a pinch of saffron in a dessert with oranges or lemons for something a bit more unusual.

Sage

An ancient herb, thought to be good for the skin and a natural antiseptic. The leaves can be quite large. They're a muted, forest-green colour and slightly grainy and textured, with one side usually paler in colour than the other. The leaves are incredible when picked off the stem and fried in oil for a minute or two on each side until they turn crisp and dark. The frying seems to concentrate their earthy, clean flavour. Save the scented oil and trickle it over your dish or dress a salad with it. Sage is traditionally served with chicken or pork, but it's also very good with turkey. Despite its appearance, sage isn't as delicate as some of the other herbs - it can withstand some cooking. Depending on how long you cook it, it will either soften in the pan (like it does when making a minced meat hash) or will turn crisp and crunchy when fried in oil or roasted. Try it with sweet potatoes and squash, too.

Salt

Salt isn't a herb or a spice but a mineral. However, it wouldn't be right to leave it out here, because of the flavour it lends to any dish. And while we often think of adding salt to our savoury dishes, sweet dishes can benefit from a pinch of salt, too. In fact, it can trick our tastebuds into imagining a dessert is actually sweeter. Try it, as I've done for my Chai Tea Cake with Salted Chai Frosting. For best results, and a better flavour that tastes just like the sea, go for sea salt. You can buy flakes, crystals or ground salt ready to serve. I actually love some texture in salt, it lends a crunch to sweet potato fries or roasted meats. Pink Himalayan salt is also available. You can also buy smoked salt, which adds a beautiful, slightly charred flavour to marinades and rubs.

Tarragon

Up until recently, I'd never been much of a fan of tarragon, if I'm honest. And then I ate it chopped in a sardine salad and fell in love with it. Often used in French cooking, the leaves are delicate and have a strong, aromatic, aniseed flavour. It has been most often used as a partner to chicken but you can also eat it with oily fish, including sardines and mackerel. Tarragon is also great with lamb - in my ebook *AIP and Paleo Snacks and Quick Lunches* I made a beautiful lamb and tarragon burger recipe that we eat quite often at home. The clean aniseed from the leaves cuts any fattiness from the lamb and lifts the flavour. Fresh tarragon can be hard to come by for me, so I often use dried tarragon in its place. You still get the aromatic aniseed, but the flavour is slightly more muted and less vibrant.

Thyme

Like rosemary, thyme is another woody herb. It has small, thin woody stems and tiny, fragile-looking green leaves. Give the stems a wash and just run your finger down the stem in the opposite direction of the leaf growth and the leaves will fall off onto your board or roasting dish. Thyme has a very aromatic, fragrant and sweet flavour. It's amazing with mushrooms, roasted meats and pairs well with rosemary and bay. It's also great with beef and lamb. I always keep a pot of dried thyme on hand and sprinkle over vegetables before roasting. It's also a good herb to use to make spice rubs and powders.

Turmeric

Turmeric comes in two types: fresh and ground. Fresh turmeric is a pale golden, knobbly root that looks a bit like a spindly ginger root, but slightly more orange in colour. Cut into it though, and you'll see a dark orange colour that will stain pretty much anything it touches. When I first started using fresh turmeric, a friend gave me a long list of all the things I could do with it, before adding: "wear gloves". Fresh turmeric has a zesty, sweet flavour that's similar to ginger but much less strong and spicy. It is aromatic and earthy and can be chopped and added to stir-fries, or grated and stirred into dishes. It can also be frozen - freeze in a freeze-proof container and take out a piece when needed, grating it straight from the freezer. If you defrost it and leave it at room temperature before using, I've found it can turn soft and soggy and difficult to chop. I almost always use the ground version in my dishes. Again - it stains, so be careful - but the dried powder is much easier to add a spoonful to a curry paste or smoothie, as you need it.

Vanilla

There's no mistaking the heady tones of vanilla. In fact, some studies have shown that it could work as an aphrodisiac. In this book, I've used vanilla extract - and not the seeds or pods, which aren't AIP compliant - but you can also use vanilla powder if you can get hold of it. Vanilla extract (buy the best quality you can) is AIP-compliant if it's gluten-free and heated in the recipe. It can contain some alcohol and this is burned off during cooking. For strict AIP, don't use vanilla paste - this black paste contains the pod and the seeds - at least not until you've reintroduced them successfully.

Watercress

Watercress is more of a vegetable than a herb, I know. But it has such a strong, peppery flavour that I often use it in recipes instead of pepper. It's also incredibly nutrient dense, and is my choice of salad leaf just so I can up my nutrient intake for the day. It's high in Vitamin C and Vitamin A, so it's a good choice to have in the fridge. Serve watercress with salmon as well as other types of fish, and beef. You can also blitz it up into a Green-Goddess style dressing, as I've done in the book.

So, How Do You Make A Curry Without Seeds or Nightshades?

To begin with, making authentic curries without seeds, nuts and nightshades was quite challenging as they're such an integral part of most curries. Ground almonds often thicken a regular, non AIP curry sauce, while seed spices give a deep, savoury flavour, so I

had to look for alternatives. Nightshades usually provide colour and spice - as in the case of fresh tomato, paprika or chilli powder.

After you've completed the initial strict elimination stage of AIP and gone through your reintroductions, feel free to tinker the recipes with ingredients you've found you can tolerate. Re-introduced seeds? Drop in a couple of cardamom pods for a rounded, almost citrus flavour to your Indian dish. Found out you're fine with nightshades? Then add chilli powder, paprika or chopped green or red chillies to your curry. I wanted to keep all the recipes here compliant with the strict elimination phase of AIP though, because that's the point where it becomes most challenging to create gorgeous tasting curries without all of these things. And you can totally get around it.

The formula below is meant as a rough guide - insert your own favourite spices and herbs here as you experiment. For example, horseradish root will add heat and can be added to a recipe along with the base aromatics. Coconut yoghurt serves as a good, tangy, creamy base when you want a drier, less liquid sauce, or for marinades.

THE FORMULA FOR AN AIP CURRY

CHOOSE YOUR BASE AROMATICS	CHOOSE YOUR SAUCE BASE	EMBELLISH WITH SPICES	CHOOSE YOUR TOPPINGS
Garlic	Bone Broth/	Turmeric	Coriander Leaf
Spring Onion	Stock	Cloves	Shredded
Onion	Coconut Milk	Cinnamon	Coconut
Ginger	Coconut Cream	Dried Coriander	Fried Onions
Lemongrass	Coconut	Leaf	Spring Onions
Basil	Yoghurt	Lemongrass	Lemon Juice
Coriander Leaf	Water		Lime Juice
	Vegetables		
	NoMato Sauce		

Indian-Style Curries

Onions

To begin with, you don't have nightshade spices and seeds like coriander seed or cumin to add a deep colour and rich, earthy flavour to your dish, so you have to use something else instead. I like to fry thinly sliced onion - preferably red onion for its sweetness - until deep brown and golden to give a rich base for a curry. You'll find that the deeper brown the onions get, the darker and richer-looking your curry will be. The onions also add that deep 'umami' flavour that seed-based spices often give, but be careful not to burn them or you'll end up with bitterness.

Vegetables

To achieve a rich tomato-like curry without nightshades, I add vegetables. They can be carrots and beetroot, to achieve an almost tomato-like sauce, or you can add other puréed vegetables instead. Adding some starchy veggies like squash and sweet potato will also thicken the sauce, so it feels more like a rich curry rather than a watery stew.

Aromatics

As well as onions, you'll need garlic and ginger. These are staple ingredients for most curry dishes and provide earthiness and fragrance. I usually add them just after I've browned the onions in the pan and fry them off quite quickly before adding the rest of the ingredients.

Herbs and Spices

I often use dried coriander leaf in my Indian-style curries, because it has a muted, earthy tone but also an element of citrus, too. It tastes completely different to fresh coriander leaf, which is often reserved for decoration or sprinkling over at the end, for colour and a fresh fragrance. As far as spices go, warm spices like cinnamon, cloves and ground ginger help round out the overall flavour of the sauce, so they're a must, but you won't need very much of each one.

Finishing Touches

Once you've made your curry, you can top with plain coriander/ cilantro leaves to lift all those dark, earthy favours with a bit of zest and fragrance. I like to top many of my curries with fried onion slices (usually red onion, again, for sweetness as well as colour). If after the strict elimination stage of AIP you have reintroduced chillies (a nightshade) you can fry slices in a little oil (coconut or avocado oil is good) until sizzling and golden and scatter them over the top of your curry, along with the oil they were cooked in. This works well for green as well as red chillies, but only if you find you can tolerate them after strict AIP. For fish and seafood curries, a wedge or two of lemon works well squeezed over, to give extra vibrance to the dish. What you decide to top your curry with depends on you tasting it and then looking for ways to balance the sweet, sour, fresh and fragrant flavours to your liking.

Thai-Style Curries

Curry Paste
You'll need a basic Thai curry paste to get you started. Obviously there are no nightshade or seed spices in the ones I use in this book, but if you find after your initial elimination phase of AIP that you can tolerate them, youcan add them if you like. The main components of an AIP-compliant Thai curry paste are ginger, garlic, lemongrass, lime, coriander leaf/cilantro, basil leaf and spring onions. Think bright, vibrant, citrussy and refreshing flavours. I like to add a spoonful of ground turmeric too for body and to lift the other flavours. Here, there are recipes for both a green and red AIP-compliant Thai curry paste.

Coconut Milk and Liquids
Once you've fried off your curry paste and it's aromatic and sizzling, you can add coconut milk to create a typical Thai curry. If you want a thicker sauce, add coconut cream instead of milk. For a thinner soup-like broth, thin the coconut sauce out with some chicken or vegetable broth or stock. If you're after a thick marinade, then use coconut yoghurt. A small dash of fish sauce

can add saltiness to a Thai-flavoured curry, if you have some handy.

Finishing Touches

I love my Thai curries with fresh coriander/cilantro leaves scattered over. You could also serve a lime wedge alongside for squeezing. And although a traditional Thai curry is served with rice, I find that serving with a cauliflower or other vegetable-based rice alternative doesn't quite work with the Thai flavours. So I always add some vegetable noodles usually made from parsnips, carrots or courgettes (zucchini) instead.

Chinese Flavours

Soy sauce is not allowed on AIP, although you could use coconut aminos if you can get hold of it. It's not easy to get hold of where I live, so I found that if you stir fry some bacon and mushrooms together, the resulting salty-umami flavour does resemble the flavour of soy sauce. So just add chopped smoked bacon and sliced mushrooms to your stir-fry for a similar flavour.

Spring onions, garlic and ginger are essential for recreating the fresh flavours of Oriental dishes. Chinese Five Spice is a blend of spices including star anise, which is eliminated in the first, strict stages of AIP. In the meantime, use fresh vegetables stir-fried with ginger, spring onions and garlic and you'll achieve an authentic flavour. To add sourness to a dish, add apple cider vinegar or tamarind paste, which gives a silky, bitter taste. Sweetness and stickiness can be added using runny honey.

You can try reintroducing Chinese staple ingredients like chillies and sesame seeds after you complete the initial 'calming down' stage of the autoimmune protocol, but until then, you can absolutely enjoy the AIP equivalent of a Chinese takeaway complete with crispy seaweed, sweet and sour sauce and stir-fries.

About the Recipes

All recipes were created using metric measurements. I've converted them where possible, as best I can, but if in any doubt, go for the metric measurement.

I don't use a lot of AIP-compliant flours in my cooking, because I've found they're quite hard to buy where I live. I mainly use tapioca flour, arrowroot powder and coconut flour.

A note on oil - use any preferred oil or fat that you usually use for your cooking. I generally use a mild, unflavoured coconut oil, but you can use your favourite.

Coriander/Cilantro: In the UK, where I live, coriander is the name of both the seed spice and the leaf of the plant. Coriander leaf (or cilantro, as it's also known) is AIP compliant, but the seed of the plant (ground coriander/coriander seeds) is not. When I mention coriander in recipes, I'm referring only to the leaf.

Many of the ingredients can be bought at large supermarkets or, in some cases, even the corner shop - but if you're struggling to find ingredients then have a look in health stores.

If you make any of the recipes here I'd love to see them! You can post your photos to social media - I can be found on Twitter and Instagram @joromerofood. Use the hashtag #AIPSPICE and I'll share any that I see.

Nibbles and Soups

One of the things about healthy eating is that you can't just grab a packet of crisps if you're hungry or stuff pastries into your mouth at a party. So it's always good to have a few nibbles or snacks up your sleeve. You basically need something quick to eat, to satisfy your hunger. Party foods can be special and indulgent and may take some planning and putting together, but soups are also ideal. You just make up a batch and reheat a ladleful or two when you need it.

In this chapter there are Thai, Chinese and Indian-inspired soups. Have some fun with the herbs and spices and create your own flavour blends. You'll really look forward to a soothing, aromatic bowl that refreshes and bolsters you.

The snacks and nibbles in this chapter can be brought out as party foods - or quickly made and eaten standing up at the kitchen worktop, off the baking tray, as I have often done.

Fragrant Herb and Coconut Chicken Soup

This was one of the first AIP-compliant recipes I created, and it was probably the first recipe that got me thinking about how to use spices and herbs on the autoimmune protocol. It's soothing and rich, with flavours of lemongrass, ginger and coriander. Fresh, fruity basil leaves lift and round out the other flavours, giving you a very aromatic and comforting soup. Feel free to add more lime juice or salt to balance the flavours for you. Turkey, pork, fish and seafood are also good with this soup in place of chicken - just adjust the cooking times accordingly. Serves 3-4.

For the paste:
2 sliced lemongrass stalks
2 fat garlic cloves, peeled
1cm (about half an inch) slice of fresh ginger, peeled
3 spring onions, washed and trimmed
small handful fresh coriander/cilantro (use the stalks for the paste)
juice of half a lime
handful of fresh basil, stalks and all
good pinch of salt

For the soup:
2 ladlefuls of home-made chicken stock or broth
400ml (14 fl oz) can coconut milk
1 tsp coconut oil
4 large chestnut mushrooms, sliced
big handful leftover roasted shredded chicken
1 courgette (zucchini), top and tailed and sliced into strips using a vegetable peeler

Method

Blitz the ingredients for the paste in a food processor, saving the coriander/cilantro leaves for scattering over after cooking the soup (use the stalks to make the paste). Next, melt the 1 tsp coconut oil in a medium-sized saucepan and fry the paste for a couple of minutes until sizzling and aromatic. Pour in the chicken stock and the coconut milk and bring to a simmer, stirring to incorporate all the herbs and spices.

Once the soup base is simmering nicely, add the cooked chicken, mushrooms and courgette strips and continue to cook for another 5 minutes, until everything is warmed through and hot throughout. Taste, and season with more salt if needed. Serve in bowls, with the coriander/cilantro leaves scattered over and a wedge of lime.

Garlic Plantain Chips with Zesty Guacamole

These crunchy plantain chips take minutes to make - they're best served crisp and slightly warm, with the zesty guacamole alongside. Just make sure you slice the plantain chips thinly, otherwise they don't crispen up the same. And do use green plantains - yellow or greenish-yellow will taste sweeter and not quite right in this recipe. Serves 3-4.

For the plantains:
1 tbsp mild unflavoured coconut or avocado oil
3 large green plantains
1/4 tsp garlic salt or garlic powder

For the guacamole:
2 ripe avocados
juice of 1 lime
pinch of salt

chopped coriander leaf (optional)
finely chopped red onion (optional)

Method
First, make the guacamole. Peel and take the stone out of each avocado. Mash the flesh roughly in a bowl using a fork and squeeze in the juice of the lime. Give it all a stir and add the salt, along with the chopped coriander and red onion if using. Put to one side while you make the plantain chips.

Peel the plantains and slice them thinly. Heat the coconut or avocado oil in a large frying pan until hot and then add the plantain slices in one layer. Fry for a minute or two on each side until golden and just crisp. Lift the slices out onto a piece of kitchen towel to drain and fry the rest of the slices in batches if necessary. Don't over-crowd the pan, or the plantain chips might go soggy and not crispen up. Dust the warm plantain chips with the garlic salt and serve immediately, with the guacamole.

Mushroom and Fennel Soup

I love how the fennel lifts the deep, earthy 'umami' flavour of the mushrooms in the soup. Use the bulb, but add in any feathery leaves after blending, for extra aniseed flavour and some colour contrast. Serves 4.

half teaspoon of cooking oil or cooking fat of your choice
1 small white onion, peeled and roughly chopped
350g (12oz) chestnut mushrooms, trimmed and cleaned
1 medium-sized bulb of fennel, cleaned and trimmed
400ml (14 fl oz.) chicken stock
pinch of salt

Method

Heat the oil in a medium-sized saucepan and gently fry the onion until just softened. Quickly chop the mushrooms and add them to the pan, stirring until they begin to darken and soften. Chop the fennel bulb into 2-3cm pieces and add these to the mushrooms and onion, gently frying on a low heat, for 2-3 minutes. Pour in the stock and simmer gently for 5-10 minutes, until everything is heated through and the fennel is soft. Blend until smooth. Taste and add salt to season. Serve hot.

Spicy Broccoli and Ginger Soup

Greens pair perfectly with spicy, fragrant ginger in this nutrient-dense soup. Don't throw away the stalks - blend them up in the pan for a richer, creamier texture to the soup. The end result is a spicy soup that has a pepperiness similar to that of black pepper. Serves 3-4.

1 tsp mild, unflavoured coconut oil
2 cloves garlic, peeled and chopped
1 large white onion, peeled and chopped
2 tbsp chopped fresh ginger
330g (11 oz) broccoli, including the stalks
500ml (2 cups) chicken broth or stock
pinch of salt, to taste

Method
Heat the oil in a medium-sized saucepan and add the garlic, onion and ginger, stir-frying until slightly softened and aromatic. Chop up the broccoli and add it, including the chopped stalk, to the pan. Pour over the stock or broth and simmer for 15 minutes or so until the broccoli is tender - the stalks will take the longest to cook.

Blend until smooth and then taste, seasoning with salt as needed. Serve hot.

AIP Ginger and Salmon Sushi Maki Rolls

Rather than the usual cauliflower rice, which is a popular altern-ative to grains, I've chopped courgette (zucchini) which is mild in flavour and picks up whatever flavours you're cooking it with. It's also a low-FODMAP option. My courgette pieces are still rather large in the picture, feel free to chop them smaller, or use a food processor to help you - it will help the sushi roll better. Makes 6 maki rolls.

1 sheet of dried nori
1 tsp mild, unflavoured coconut oil
1 medium sized courgette, ends trimmed and the courgette finely chopped (see note above)
1 tsp freshly grated ginger root
1 cooked salmon fillet
avocado slices (optional)
Method
Lay the nori sheet out on a bamboo sushi rolling mat, with the shiny side facing down.

Heat the oil in a frying pan and fry the courgette pieces with the ginger until softened, but still fairly firm. This will take about 60 seconds or so. Turn off the heat, tip the courgette out onto a plate and leave to cool completely.

Once the courgette 'rice' has cooled, spread it out over the nori sheet, leaving a gap at the bottom and top. Break the salmon fillet into pieces or slice it into strips and lay it out along the bottom of the mat, left to right. Add some thin avocado slices here if you want to.

To roll, lift the mat up from the bottom and roll it over the salmon filling. Continue to press down and roll the bamboo mat (and the nori sheet with it) until you have a tightly-rolled cylinder. Transfer the sushi to a board and, using a sharp knife, cut it into slices. Serve straight away, or refrigerate until serving.

AIP Chinese Beef Noodle Soup

A warming, Chinese-style noodle (or should I say 'zoodle') soup, topped with sliced beef and packed with healing bone broth and vegetables. Sounds perfect. And it'll be on the table in around 10 minutes or less. Serves 2.

1 large steak (ribeye, sirloin, rump)
1 tsp coconut oil
pinch of salt
350ml (one and a half cups) beef broth or stock
1 large courgette and 1 large carrot trimmed and spiralized (or cut into ribbons using a potato peeler or julienne peeler)
1 cm (about half an inch) chunk fresh ginger root, peeled
1 garlic clove, peeled
3 spring onions

Method

First, cook the steak. Season it with salt and grill or fry on a medium-high heat, turning half-way through cooking, until cooked to your liking. Put to one side, to rest, while you get on with the soup.

Next, pour the broth into a large saucepan and bring to a gentle simmer. Drop in the courgette and carrot noodles, finely grate in the ginger root and garlic cloves and chop and add two of the spring onions.

Continue to cook, until the broth is hot and the vegetable noodles are just tender.

Slice the steak into strips. Using tongs, lift the vegetables out of the saucepan and into warmed bowls, pouring the broth over the top. Place the steak slices on top and sprinkle over the remaining chopped spring onion, to serve. Eat straight away.

Creamy Carrot and Lemongrass Soup

The zesty lemongrass stalk gives this sweet carrot soup a beautiful, almost spicy, Thai-like flavour. It's one of my absolute favourite soups, and because it's smooth, sweet and soothing, it's perfect for breakfast as well as lunch or dinner. I make this differently from my Thai style curry pastes - I split the lemongrass stalk and leave it in the soup to infuse its beautiful, uplifting fragrance, and then I lift it out. Lemongrass can have quite a coarse texture unless you have a very powerful blender so it helps make this soup very smooth and comforting - with no bits. Serves 2-3 (makes 2 big mugfuls)

1 tbsp mild, unflavoured coconut oil
1 small onion, peeled and chopped roughly
1 garlic clove, peeled and chopped roughly
1 chunky slice of fresh ginger, peeled and chopped (the slice should be about half a centimetre thick)
400g (14 oz) carrots, trimmed and washed (and peeled if you like)
250ml (1 cup) chicken broth or vegetable stock
dash of full fat coconut milk
1 lemongrass stalk

Method
First, melt the coconut oil on a gentle heat in a medium saucepan. Add the onion and the garlic and fry for a minute or two until fragrant and sizzling. Add the ginger and then the chopped carrots and stir everything together. Pour in the stock or broth and splash in the coconut milk - you'll need a dash - about half a cup's worth.

Next, put the lemongrass stalk on a board and peel off any scruffy outer layer, if there is one. Give it a rinse under the tap and then, using a sharp knife, cut a split along the middle of the stalk, all the way down, vertically, but don't cut all the way though. Drop the lemongrass stalk into the pan with the other ingredients and push it down under the surface of the liquid. Leave to simmer gently for about 20 minutes, or until the carrots are tender.

Once the carrots are cooked through, lift the lemongrass stalk out of the soup and then blend until smooth, adding some more coconut milk for a creamier consistency, if you like.

Spring Greens Soup with Basil Oil

This soup is packed with greens - I use spring greens, but any leafy green cabbage would work well, too. You get the healing broth along with the veggies - and a trickle of basil oil swirled over the top lifts it all with its fruity, sweet flavour. It's a quick soup to make, too - ready in around 15 minutes. Serves 3-4.

1 tsp preferred cooking fat or oil
1 clove garlic, peeled and chopped
1 head of spring greens/cabbage, washed and sliced
1 large leek, washed, trimmed and sliced
500ml (2 cups) chicken stock or broth
pinch of salt, if needed
1 tbsp basil oil, or to taste

Method
First, melt the fat or oil in a large saucepan and add the chopped garlic, sliced greens and the sliced leek. Let everything sizzle together for a minute or two and then pour in the broth. Bring it to a simmer and cook for 10 minutes or so, until the greens and leeks are soft. Blend until smooth. Taste and season with a pinch of salt if you think it needs it. Ladle into bowls and drizzle over the basil oil just before serving.

Indian-Style Sweet Potato Patties

These sweet potato cakes really look the part. You can use any leftover sweet potato mash to make them, or add an extra sweet potato to the oven when you're baking up a few for dinner. With turmeric, cloves and coriander leaves, they're aromatic and delicately spiced. Serve with lime wedges for squeezing over. Any leftovers can be reheated the next day. Makes 4.

1 medium sweet potato, baked and cooled, skin discarded
pinch of garlic salt (or garlic powder + a small pinch of salt)

pinch of ground cloves
half teaspoon turmeric
1 spring onion, washed, trimmed and snipped into small pieces
handful coarsely grated root vegetables (parsnip, carrot or swede
are all good)
1 tbsp fresh coriander/cilantro leaves, plus more for sprinkling on
afterwards, if you like
1 tsp preferred cooking fat or oil (I used mild, unflavoured
coconut oil)

Method
In a bowl, mix together the cooled, cooked sweet potato flesh
with the garlic salt, cloves, turmeric, spring onion, root veg and
coriander leaves. Mix until evenly combined.

Heat the cooking fat or oil in a saucepan. Pick up a quarter of the
mixture and drop gently into the frying pan. Repeat with the other
quarters so you have four patties sizzling away. As they cook,
shape them with the spatula you're using into patty-shapes. Once
golden on one side (about 5 minutes), carefully slide the spatula
underneath the patties and flip them over to cook on the other
side. Once the other side is golden and the patties are cooked
through, serve straight away with more coriander/cilantro leaves
scattered over and wedges of lime for squeezing as you eat.

AIP Onion Bhajis

*And I never thought this was possible. In fact, it took me quite a
few tries to get this right, as you don't have egg (or floury batter)
to help keep the bhajis together as they're frying. The secret is to
use thinly-sliced onions and not to disturb them while they're
cooking in the pan. Let them crispen up first, and use fairly hot
oil. Resist the urge to keep stirring and prodding them, until
they're golden on the first side - then flip them over. I've added a
warm, Indian-style spice mix and a little tapioca flour and they're*

great. These bhajis fry up really quickly and they're beautiful served up with some lemon juice and a sprinkling of sea salt. You can also serve them with a drizzle of Indian Mint Dip (see section on Sauces) if you like. If you wanted to, rather than make these as bhajis, you could also just create a stir-fried onion dish by stir-frying them all in one go rather than forming into individual bhajis. Recipe makes about 6 onion bhajis.

1 medium-sized red onion
1 medium-sized white onion
1 tsp turmeric
half teaspoon ground ginger
1 tbsp dried coriander/cilantro leaf
quarter teaspoon ground cloves
1 tsp tapioca flour
1 tsp preferred cooking fat (I used mild, unflavoured coconut oil)
salt and lemon wedges, to serve

Method
Peel the onions and carefully slice them as thinly as you can. Tumble the onion slices into a bowl and add the turmeric, ginger, coriander/cilantro leaf, ground cloves and tapioca flour. Give everything a good stir to coat the onion rings well in the spices.

Heat the oil or fat in a frying pan and take small handfuls of the tangled onion mixture. Drop them into the pan, spacing them apart, and fry for 2-3 minutes on one side. When the onion has started to turn crisp and golden, slide the spatula underneath the bhaji and quickly flip them over to cook on the other side. Try to resist the urge to fiddle with them too much, as they can break up. Once they're golden and slightly crisp on the other side, lift them onto a sheet of paper towel to drain and then serve them straight away, while hot - with a sprinkling of salt and lemon juice on the side.

Sweet Potato, Spring Onion and Ginger Soup

I love this soup. It's spicy, thanks to the ginger, as well as soothing - and has a thick, velvety texture. It's pretty easy to make, too. Serves 3.

400ml (14 fl. oz) chicken (or vegetable) broth or stock
2 medium-sized sweet potatoes, peeled and chopped into bite-sized chunks
2 spring onions, washed, trimmed and chopped (plus one extra, to serve)
1 small piece of fresh ginger, about the size of your thumb—peeled and chopped
salt to season, if necessary

Method
Heat the chicken stock in a medium-sized saucepan and drop in the sweet potato chunks, the 2 chopped spring onions and the chopped ginger. Bring everything to a simmer and cook for 10 minutes, or until the sweet potato pieces are tender. Blend until smooth, adding a little water if you need to loosen it slightly. Taste and season with a little salt if you think it needs it.

Chop the remaining spring onion and scatter it over the soup just before serving.

Tuna, Palm Heart and Coriander Salad

I first ate palm hearts in Argentina, where they slice them up lengthways and strew over the top of pizza. I fell in love with them, there and then. Nowadays, I've ditched the oozy pizza, but enjoy palm hearts in salads and on meat pizzas (or Meatzzas). They're surprisingly nutritious, being a good source of potassium and vitamin B6. Try them in this tuna salad, paired with fresh coriander leaves to add a zesty fragrance. Serves 1.

1 little gem lettuce, trimmed, washed and finely sliced
half a celery stick, washed, trimmed and sliced
3 radishes, washed, trimmed and sliced
1 palm heart stick, from a can, sliced
half a 150g can tuna
small handful of coriander/cilantro leaves, roughly chopped
1 tbsp extra virgin olive oil
juice of half a lime
pinch of salt
avocado slices, to serve

Method
Add the little gem lettuce, celery, radishes and palm heart slices to a serving bowl. Scatter in the canned tuna and top with the coriander/cilantro leaves. Drizzle with the olive oil and the lime juice and season with a pinch of salt if needed. Serve with avocado slices too, if you like.

Main Meals

So this is the main event. The meals you crave after a long day at work, or dinners you want to make and share with friends. You'll find slow-cook meals as well as quick ones that you can put together easily. There are AIP compliant curries with different flavour combinations, and dishes inspired by Indian, Thai and Egyptian foods, too, so you can get experimenting with herbs and spices.

When I was developing the recipes for this chapter, I changed the way I cooked and planned my meals. I took a spice or a herb and thought about which meat, fish or vegetables would work with it best, rather than the other way around. It's a fun activity and you'll probably come up with some unusual combinations. Here, the spices and herbs take centre stage.

Thai Inspired Turkey Meatball Curry

This is one of the most popular recipes on the blog and I had to include it here, as the book wouldn't be quite complete without it. A fragrant bowl of Thai-inspired coconut sauce flavoured with lemongrass, basil, coriander and garlic with light turkey meatballs and courgette strips served on top. Comforting, nourishing and plain delicious. Use pork, seafood or chicken in place of the turkey meatballs, if you like. Serves 4.

2 sticks of lemongrass, sliced
2 cloves of garlic, peeled and roughly chopped
big handful fresh coriander/cilantro leaf
handful fresh basil leaves
juice of half a lime
1 cm (about half an inch) thick slice of ginger
400g (14oz) turkey thigh mince
1 tsp coconut oil
2 spring onions (green onions), finely chopped
pinch of salt
2 courgettes (zucchinis), trimmed and peeled into strips with a
vegetable peeler
400ml (14 fl oz) coconut milk
quarter tsp turmeric

Method
First, make the curry paste. Put the lemongrass, garlic, basil and
ginger and lime juice in a small food processor. Cut the stalks off
the coriander/cilantro bunch and add these in too, reserving the
leaves for later. Blitz it all up until you get a citrus-smelling,
greenish paste. Put to one side.

Gently fry the sliced spring onion in a little coconut oil until
slightly softened. Put to one side to cool. Once cooled, combine
with the turkey mince and the pinch of salt in a bowl until just
mixed and form into small bite-sized meatballs. Brown them in
the pan for about 5 minutes, turning regularly and then transfer to
a baking tray and bake in the oven at 200°C/gas mark 6/400°F for
about 10-15 minutes, or until cooked through.

To make the sauce, tip the curry paste into the frying pan (I use
the same frying pan all the way through) and fry gently until
aromatic and sizzling. Pour in the coconut milk and then add the
courgette/zucchini strips and then the turmeric. Simmer for a few

minutes, until everything has warmed through and the courgettes are soft. Taste and season with a little more salt if you need to.

Serve the meatballs with the sauce, with freshly-chopped coriander leaves sprinkled on top.

Roasted King Prawns With Smoked Garlic, Coriander and Lime

One of our favourites. Even my kids love to dig in and peel the prawns, although they sometimes need a bit of help. The prawns don't take long to cook - around 20 minutes - and because they're cooked in the shell they're protected by the heat of the oven and stay juicy and tender without over-cooking. The smoked garlic gives the dish a subtle bonfire-like flavour. If you can't get hold of smoked garlic, use regular garlic instead. Beautiful. Serves 3.

2 tsp coconut oil
10-12 raw welfare-farmed King Prawns, shell-on
2 cloves smoked garlic (or regular garlic), chopped
large handful fresh parsley, chopped
small handful fresh coriander leaves/cilantro, chopped
pinch of salt
1 lime (plus more for serving if you like)

Method
First, preheat your oven to gas mark 6/200°C. Get out a roasting dish and add the coconut oil, sliding it in to the oven to melt - just for about 2 minutes.

Once the oil has melted, take out the dish and throw in the prawns, in a single layer. In a bowl, stir together the chopped garlic, parsley and coriander leaves/cilantro and squeeze in the juice of a lime. Season with salt and then toss the prawns in this mixture, give the dish a shake and roast in the oven for 20 minutes, until the shells are a golden shade of coral and the juices are sizzling.

Serve the prawns hot, with extra lime wedges for squeezing over if you want to.

Bacon Beef Burgers with Rocket Chimichurri

I am so in love with this creamy version of chimichurri. Plus, because it has rocket (arugula) leaves in it it's peppery, a brighter green and full of nutrients. I read once that the Romans used to think that there were tiny insects that lived on rocket leaves that used to bite you on the tongue when you ate the leaves. We know that's not true, but it does show that even the ancient Romans enjoyed the taste of this spicy, peppery plant. The salsa works so well with the beef, which is given a smoky flavour thanks to the bacon. Win. Serves 4.

For the burgers:
3 slices smoked streaky bacon, chopped into small pieces
400g (14oz) minced beef
pinch or two of salt

For the rocket chimichurri:
large handful of fresh rocket (arugula) leaves
small handful fresh parsley (should give you about 3 tbsp, chopped)
1 large garlic clove, peeled and roughly chopped
2 tsp apple cider vinegar
5 tbsp extra virgin olive oil

Method
First, make the burgers. Fry the bacon pieces until golden and quite crisp and put to one side. If your bacon is fatty enough you won't need any extra fat or oil to do this, the fat should render down from the bacon.

Once the bacon pieces are cool, mix them with the beef mince and form into 4 large patties. Season each with a sprinkle of salt, as you would season a steak, and then fry in the pan you just cooked the bacon in. The fat left in the pan will add more flavour.

While the burgers are cooking, make the chimichurri. Blend the rocket leaves, parsley, peeled garlic clove, apple cider vinegar and extra virgin olive oil with a pinch of salt, until smooth and creamy.

Flip the burgers over and cook on the other side, until cooked through, and serve them with the salsa.

Mutton and Spinach Curry

Mutton is a much under-rated meat. It has a similar flavour to lamb, only richer and deeper. It doesn't have the tenderness of lamb though, because it comes from an older animal that's worked its muscles for a bit longer so you need to cook it slowly to get the best results. This isn't a spicy curry, but it is rich and full-flavoured. It gets its colour from the onions, which are cooked until they're a deep brown colour before the rest of the ingredients are added. You can make this in a casserole dish in the oven or in the slow cooker.

Serves 4
Ingredients
2 tbsp mild, flavourless coconut oil or lard
1 white onion, peeled and chopped
2 garlic cloves, peeled and chopped roughly
thumb-sized piece of ginger, peeled and chopped
pinch of salt
400g (14 oz) mutton, diced (you could use lamb or goat, instead, if that's what you have handy)
1 tsp turmeric
large handful (about 100g) fresh spinach leaves
3 heaped tablespoons coconut yoghurt
1 red onion, peeled and sliced
Coriander/cilantro leaves, to serve

Method
Melt 1 tablespoon of the coconut oil in a large frying pan and fry
the onion until it's quite well-browned. I usually leave mine until
each piece is tinged golden-brown at the edges. Throw in the
garlic and ginger, followed by a pinch of salt and stir-fry for a
minute or so until it's aromatic.

Add the mutton pieces and stir so that the meat gets evenly
browned. Add the turmeric and the spinach leaves. Once the
leaves have wilted down, stir in 2 tablespoons of the coconut
yoghurt. Add a splash of water and transfer either to the crockpot
of your slow cooker (cook on high for 3-4 hours) or into a
casserole dish with a lid (cook in the oven for 2-3 hours on low).

Just before serving (take a look at the mutton and squish a piece
with the back of a spoon - it'll be meltingly tender) fry the onion
slices in the remaining tablespoon of coconut oil until just golden.
Taste the curry and adjust for seasoning, adding more salt and
another spoonful of coconut yoghurt or a splash more water if
needed, and stir through. Serve with the onion rings scattered
over the top and a good handful of the coriander leaves.

Lamb and Saffron Stew

*There's a dish in Azerbaijan called Plov where lamb is cooked
until tender with spices, dried fruits and served with rice. I made
it once and loved it - and I knew when this book was in the
planning stage that I wanted to create something similar, so I
made a stew with similar flavours. There's earthy saffron, sweet
apricots and prunes, and warmth from the cloves and cinnamon.
If you're after something a bit different to your usual lamb stew,
this is a perfect one-pot meal. You can serve it with your favourite
vegetable rice or mash, if you like. Serves 3-4.*

1 tsp mild, flavourless coconut oil
500g (1lb) boneless lamb leg, diced
3 garlic cloves, peeled and chopped
1 red onion, peeled and chopped
3 medium carrots, peeled and chopped
small handful each of dried apricots and dried prunes
400ml (14 fl. oz) beef broth or stock
small pinch of saffron threads
pinch of ground cloves
pinch of ground cinnamon
salt, to taste
freshly chopped parsley, to serve (optional)

Method
Melt the coconut oil in a fairly large saucepan and brown the lamb until sealed on all sides and turning golden. Add the garlic, onion and carrots and stir well to mix, before adding the apricots and prunes. Pour in the broth or stock and then add the saffron, cloves and cinnamon. Turn the heat down and cook gently for 20-25 minutes, until the lamb is tender. Taste and season with salt before serving - you can sprinkle with chopped fresh parsley to help lift all those warm flavours, too.

Honey Ginger Stir-Fried Beef with Cabbage

This is what I cook when I get a craving for a Chinese takeaway. It takes just a few minutes to put together, so I reckon it's even quicker (as well as healthier) than ordering takeout from your local restaurant. There's no soy in the recipe - instead the ginger takes centre stage and its zesty flavour contrasts well with the beef and cabbage. A weeknight winner. Serves 2-3.

1 tsp mild, unflavoured coconut oil (or use lard or bacon fat to make this coconut-free)
2 x ribeye steaks

4 large Savoy cabbage leaves,
1 large clove garlic, peeled
1 thumb-sized piece of fresh ginger, peeled
4 spring onions, washed, trimmed and sliced
Good pinch of salt
2 tsp runny honey

Method

First, heat the coconut oil (or whatever fat you're using) in a large frying pan or wok. Cut the steaks into thin strips, trimming away any tough bits as you go, and add to the pan.

Stir-fry the beef until browned on the outside. Quickly remove the thick, white part of the cabbage leaves and then shred them fairly finely. Throw them into the pan and then grate in the garlic and ginger. Add the spring onions and the pinch of salt. The steak should be cooked - once it is, and the cabbage is tender, turn off the heat. Drizzle the honey into the pan and serve hot.

Indian Style Whole Roast Chicken

We love this version of roast chicken, changed up with spices and herbs for an Indian flavour. The marinade is stirred together with coconut yoghurt, so that it creates a Tandoori-like crust over the meat as it cooks. If you're looking for something a bit different for a weekend lunch, this is perfect. You can also use the marinade for chicken wings - just slather it over the wings and roast them

50

for 25-30 minutes, or until crisp-skinned and thoroughly cooked through. If you have any leftovers, they're great chopped up and served in a crunchy salad. Serves 4-6.

1 clove garlic, peeled and grated
1 tsp ginger, grated
1 heaped teaspoon ground turmeric
2 tbsp coconut yoghurt
zest and juice from 1 lemon
good pinch of salt
half teaspoon dried coriander/cilantro leaf
small pinch of ground cloves
a 1.4kg (3lb) whole chicken
lemon wedges, to serve

Method
Mix together the garlic, ginger, turmeric, coconut yoghurt, lemon zest and juice, salt, dried coriander leaf and the pinch of cloves in a small bowl. Take the chicken out of the fridge and place it on a roasting tray. Preheat the oven to gas mark 5/190°C/375°F.

Slather the marinade all over the chicken, rubbing it into the skin and leave for 10 minutes.

Roast the chicken until cooked through - about one and a half hours. Pierce the chicken at the thickest part to make sure it's fully cooked and there are no pink juices left. Once thoroughly cooked, leave the chicken to rest for 5-10 minutes and then carve and serve straight away.

Egyptian Lamb Artichoke Hash

A couple of years ago, a friend of mine who was studying for a degree in Egyptology gave me a book as a present. It was called Food Fit For Pharoahs by Michelle Berriedale-Johnson. I'd always been fascinated by the different types of food eaten throughout history, and I loved to flick through and learn about the flavours of ancient Egypt. One of the recipes was a tender, slow-cooked bubbling stew with lamb and artichokes, flavoured with turmeric and lemon. I became fascinated with how artichokes and lamb could work together with warm, aromatic spices and was inspired to create this meat hash, for lunch or dinner in a hurry. There's lemon and turmeric, but also red onion - as much for colour as for flavour - and the whole thing is sprinkled with parsley. Beautiful. Serves 4.

400g (14 oz) minced lamb
390g (14 oz) canned artichoke hearts, drained
2 cloves garlic, peeled and roughly chopped

a small chunk of fresh ginger, about the size of a coin - about 1cm
thick, peeled
1 tsp ground turmeric
small handful of fresh parsley
half a small red onion, peeled and finely chopped
juice of half a lemon
pinch of salt, to taste

Method
First, dry-fry the lamb in a large frying pan until browned. Add
the artichoke hearts and also the garlic, ginger and turmeric.
Continue to cook, until the lamb is cooked through and has
started to turn golden brown at the edges, and the artichokes are
hot.

To serve, sprinkle with the red onion and parsley and season with
salt, if needed. Squeeze over the lemon juice just before taking to
the table, with extra wedges of lemon for squeezing over as you
eat.

Chinese Style Sweet and Sour Tamarind Prawns

*Tamarind (I use tamarind paste here) is the fruit of a leguminous
tree - the pulpy fruit grows inside a pod. It's still AIP though,
because it's the fruit that's used in making the paste. Tamarind
paste has a slightly sour flavour, and it's used in a lot of Asian
recipes. For me, this is a perfect substitute to a Chinese takeaway.
The sweet-sour, glossy prawns taste really authentic. One of my
absolute favourites, and it cooks up in a few minutes. Serves 2.*

1 tsp mild, flavourless coconut oil, or avocado oil
2 spring onions, chopped into chunks
150g (5oz) raw, peeled prawns
1 clove garlic, peeled and chopped

a 2cm (just under 1") slice of fresh ginger, peeled and
finely chopped
one and a half tsp tamarind paste
half a tsp runny honey

Method
Melt the coconut oil in a frying
pan or wok until hot and then
fry the chopped spring onion
for a few seconds until sizzling
and beginning to take on a little
colour. Add the prawns and
then the ginger and garlic. Give
it all a stir, and mix well so it
all cooks evenly. Stir in the
tamarind paste and keep
everything moving in the pan
until the prawns are blushing
pink and cooked through. This
should all take around 5-7
minutes.

Once the prawns are cooked, and your kitchen smells incredible,
drizzle over the honey and allow it to bubble up over the rest of
the ingredients. Serve straight away. A fragrant, aromatic and
Eastern-inspired dish that's ready in less than 10 minutes.

Naan Bread Asian Chicken Pizza

*This Asian-inspired naan bread pizza uses the naan recipe in the
Sides section, but instead of being formed into individual
flatbreads, it's baked into one piece, like a pizza base, before
being strewn with toppings. This is a great recipe to use up any
leftover cooked, marinated meats or seafood, such as the Whole
Roast Chicken or the Smoked Garlic and Coriander Prawns. And*

because the flatbread keeps its firm, springy bread-like texture, it doesn't crumble or break apart when it's cut. Serves 4-6.

1 x Quantity of Naan Bread Mixture (see chapter on *Sides*)
half a teaspoon mild, unflavoured coconut oil
2 handfuls of rocket leaves
fresh coriander/cilantro leaves
1 small red onion, peeled and chopped fairly finely
couple of handfuls of leftover, cooked marinated chicken

Method
Blitz together the naan bread base as directed in the recipe and spread it out onto a baking tray lined with greaseproof paper and slightly oiled with coconut oil. Spread the dough to about 1cm thick and bake at gas mark 6/200°C/400°F for about 30 minutes, flipping it over and baking for another 10-15 minutes on the other side, or until the dough is cooked through, firm and slightly golden. Turn off the oven and leave the naan base to cool.

Once the base has cooled, transfer it to a serving board and scatter with the rocket and fresh coriander/cilantro leaves. Chop up the leftover cooked chicken and scatter this all over the top of the pizza. Top with chopped red onion, cut into pieces and serve.

Indian-Style Turkey Breakfast Hash

Sometimes, you just need something different for breakfast. Something aromatic, bolstering. Let's face it. Sometimes you just need curry, no matter what time of the day it is. I often used to eat leftover curry for breakfast alongside my bacon and eggs, so I created this AIP version of a breakfast hash you can stir together in minutes. I've used minced turkey but feel free to use chopped chicken, pork, beef or lamb if you prefer.

Serves 4
Ingredients
1 tsp preferred cooking fat or oil
350g (12oz) turkey mince
1 medium carrot, trimmed and coarsely grated
2 medium parsnips, trimmed, peeled and coarsely grated
1 medium-sized sweet potato, peeled and coarsely grated
handful of sliced green cabbage
1 clove of garlic, peeled and roughly chopped
1cm slice of ginger, peeled and roughly chopped
1 tsp ground turmeric
pinch of cloves
pinch of salt, to taste

Method
First, melt the fat in a large frying pan and brown the turkey mince until cooked through. Add in the grated carrot, parsnip and sweet potato. Stir, cooking, until the vegetables have started to soften (about 2-3 minutes) and then add the cabbage, garlic, ginger, turmeric and ground cloves. Season with a pinch of salt to taste and cook for another 5-7 minutes until all the vegetables have softened and the turkey is thoroughly cooked through. Serve straight away.

Rib-Eye Steak with Horseradish Sauce Dip

The hot spiciness of fresh horseradish root, grated into a paste and mixed with coconut cream. There's a good sprinkling of fresh parsley, too. This horseradish sauce makes a perfect dip for freshly cooked rib-eye steaks. Here I've served it with peppery watercress, rocket leaves and spinach. Serves 2.

1 tsp avocado or mild,
flavourless coconut oil
2 rib-eye steaks
pinch of salt
watercress, rocket and spinach
leaves, to serve

For the horseradish sauce:
3 heaped tbsp coconut cream
1 heaped tsp freshly finely
grated horseradish root
1 tsp finely chopped fresh
parsley
large pinch of salt
extra virgin oil, for topping

Method
Rub the steaks with the oil and season with salt. Grill or fry for 5-6 minutes, turning half way through cooking, until cooked to your liking. Take the steaks off the heat and leave to rest. While the steaks are resting, mix together the coconut cream, horseradish root, parsley and the salt. Drizzle the extra virgin olive oil over the top of the sauce before serving it with the salad leaves and the beef.

Lamb and Mint Meatball, Red Onion and Sweet Potato Bake

This is a quicker alternative to a lamb roast - and you can make it all in one tray, to save on washing up. The lamb meatballs are fragrant with fresh mint leaves and parsley. I really love the combination of sweet potato, mint and lamb - I think it works so well. Serves 4.

400g (14 oz) lamb mince
quarter teaspoon garlic powder
pinch of salt
2 tbsp chopped fresh parsley
2 tbsp chopped fresh mint leaves
1 tsp mild, unflavoured coconut oil, or avocado oil
3 large sweet potatoes, peeled and cut into wedges
1 large red onion, peeled and cut into wedges

Method
First, put the lamb mince in a bowl and add the garlic powder, salt and herbs and mix well. Pinch off small handfuls of the mixture and roll into meatballs, dropping them into a waiting frying pan as you go, that's preheated to a medium heat. Add the teaspoon of coconut oil if you need to - sometimes lamb is quite fatty and it will render down its own cooking fat.

Brown the meatballs in batches, and transfer each batch to a large roasting tray and slide into the oven at gas mark 6/200°C/400°F while you brown the rest. Add the newly-browned meatballs to this roasting tray as you go.

Once all the meatballs are browned and in the tray, turn off the stove and add the sweet potato and red onion wedges to the tray, shaking them about so they get coated in the lamb fat. Bake in the oven for about 20 minutes, until the sweet potato wedges and red onion are cooked and the lamb meatballs are heated all the way through so no pink remains. Serve hot.

Bacon-Wrapped Chimichurri Stuffed Chicken Breast

When I went to Argentina, chimichurri salsa was everywhere. And when I tried it, I was surprised for two reasons. The first was that it wasn't spicy. When I told them that the Argentine chimichurri salsa sold back home contained chopped chillies they screwed their noses up and shook their heads. Authentic chimichurri salsa isn't spicy, they told me. The second surprise was that it's eaten with a lot more than beef. Try this chimichurri-stuffed chicken breast. The parsley and garlic give the moist, tender chicken a real tang. Serves 4.

4 free-range chicken breasts
18 rashers of smoked, streaky bacon
4 teaspoons freshly made AIP compliant chimichurri salsa (see the section on *Sides*)

Method
Get your oven on to gas mark 6/200°C/400°F.

If the chicken breast still has the small strip of fillet attached, gently remove it. Then, with a sharp knife, make a cut along the side of the breast, being careful not to cut all the way through to the other side. Make the cut along the length of the breast, so you taste the chimichurri all the way through the chicken portion.

Once you've cut a pocket into the chicken, dab one teaspoonful of chimichurri onto each breast (being careful not to touch the chicken with the spoon and then stick it back in the sauce if you're saving more sauce for later). With your fingers, smear the chimichurri along the whole of the breast and then close it up, pushing the fillet in to help seal the gap, if you can.

Gently wrap with the bacon, using a couple of rashers for each breast if needed, and place on a shallow roasting tray - it helps if you make sure the loose ends of the bacon are underneath the breast so it doesn't unravel while cooking. Cook for 15 minutes and rest for 5. Cut into the chicken to make sure it's cooked - if not, put them back in for a little longer until the chicken is completely cooked through. Slice and serve hot.

Slow Cooked Lamb Shanks with Paleo Mint Sauce

This is the taste of my childhood. Lamb, usually breast of lamb, because that was the cheapest - with a fragrant bowl of home-made mint sauce to go alongside. This version is cooked in a slow cooker but you can also cook lamb shanks in liquid in a large pan on the stove or in a casserole dish in the oven. Cooking it in the slow cooker just means that I don't have to give it a second thought until dinnertime when the house smells incredible and everyone's hungry. Serves 4.

2 large lamb shanks
one large bunch of fresh mint
1-2 tsp cider vinegar
a few drops of boiling water, from the kettle

half a teaspoon of honey
salt, to taste

Method
First of all, you'll want to cook your lamb. Set your slow cooker
or crockpot to high and just drop in the lamb shanks. Replace the
lid, and cook for around 5-6 hours, or until the lamb is very
tender and falls off the bone.

Shred the meat into chunks and arrange on a serving plate.

To make the mint sauce, just pull the mint leaves off their stems,
wash them, and then chop them quite finely. Place in a bowl and
add a few drops of boiling water - just enough to moisten them.
They'll start to soften in the heat. Add a teaspoon of the apple
cider vinegar and the honey and stir. Add a pinch of salt to taste.
Have a quick taste (along with a stray piece of lamb from the
plate, if you like - 'chef's perks') and add a little more vinegar if
you think it needs it.

Serve straight away, while the lamb is still hot.

Spicy Horseradish Beets with Smoked Mackerel

If you want spicy, I'll give you spicy. As far as AIP goes, the
spiciest thing you could probably eat is either wasabi or
horseradish root - and they both come from the same family of
plants. As well as with beef, horseradish seems to pair naturally
with smoked fish really well. Here, I've just used raw horseradish
root to give a beet salad some kick and served smoked mackerel
alongside. Remember that for AIP black pepper is initially
eliminated, so choose mackerel without the black pepper topping.
Serves 2.

1 large beetroot, cooked and peeled (I buy vacuum-packed, pre-cooked beetroot for this)
a pinch of salt
about half a teaspoon of freshly grated (peeled) horseradish root
1 tbsp extra virgin olive oil
Smoked mackerel fillets, to serve

Method
Chop the beetroot and place into a bowl. Sprinkle over the salt, horseradish and drizzle over the olive oil. Mix well. Serve alongside the smoked mackerel.

Slow Cooker Thyme and Sea Salt Pulled Pork Shoulder

Pulled pork is a genius option for when you're feeding lots of people because it takes just a few seconds of actual work, and then your oven or slow cooker does the rest, while you take all the credit for delicious, tender, flavoured meat. If we have a barbecue with a lot of people, I usually stick a pork joint in the slow cooker as back up, to ease the pressure of flipping burgers and steaks outside. I've tried it with lots of different herbs, but this is my favourite way to eat it. The fresh thyme adds a kind of floral fragrance to the pork as it cooks and you just shred the meat - and the thyme sprigs along with it - and serve on a plate for everyone to dig in. This is one of my blog readers' favourite recipes and once you've tried it, you'll see why. If you get leftovers, you'll be lucky - but they're great shredded up cold, and served with sweet potato fries or in a salad with guacamole and plantain chips. Serves 6.

1.4kg (3lb) bone-in pork shoulder joint
4-5 fresh thyme sprigs
good pinch of sea salt

Method
Plug in your slow cooker and set it to 'high'. Dump the pork shoulder into the crockpot. Sprinkle with salt and give the thyme sprigs a rinse under the tap. Shake them off and strew over and around the pork. Replace the lid.

Leave to cook for 5-6 hours, or until the pork is fall-apart tender. Lift out of the crockpot (watch out as there will now be meat juices in the pot) and onto a large serving plate. Shred with two forks, leaving the thyme to shred along with the meat, and then pour over a little of the cooking juices over the top to add moisture and flavour. Serve straight away.

Pheasant Saltimbocca

You might know about the traditional Saltimbocca, a turkey steak wrapped in parma ham with a sage leaf tucked in. I decided to try this concept with pheasant. Pheasant breast is lean and quite dry if it's overcooked, and here, the bacon wrapped around it helps protect the meat from the heat of the pan. there's the smoky saltiness from the bacon - and the flavour of the sage infuses into the meat as it cooks underneath it. Serves 6 (makes 6 bacon-wrapped breasts).

6 pheasant breasts
1 tsp coconut oil (I use a mild, tasteless oil)
12 rashers of smoked, streaky bacon
12 sage leaves, washed and dried

Method
First, pick through the pheasant breasts and make sure there's a) no pieces of lead shot that you can detect and b) no fine, tufty feathers still clinging on to the meat. Give it a quick rinse under a cold tap if you like.

Lay the breasts out on a board and arrange two sage leaves over the top of each one. Carefully wrap in bacon - you'll need 2 rashers per breast. Heat the coconut oil in a large frying pan and lay the wrapped pheasant breasts into it, and fry for about 8-10 minutes, turning regularly, until they're golden on each side and thoroughly cooked through. You can cut into one to make sure, if you're in any doubt.

Transfer the cooked pheasant breasts to a plate and allow to rest for a minute or two before slicing up and serving hot.

Crispy-Skinned Chicken Breast with Porcini and Thyme Salt Crust

There's something so incredible about crispy chicken skin - it's just not the same if the skin turns soggy while cooking. And there's one way to increase your chances of crisp, golden skin on chicken - salt. I've put together a blended salt containing dried porcini mushrooms and thyme. It was made for chicken. Seriously. Serves 2.

2 chicken breast fillets, with skin-on
1 tsp *Porcini and Thyme Salt* (in *Sauces and Finishing Touches* section)

Method
This is the easiest recipe ever. Lay the chicken breast fillets out on a board or plate and dab the skin gently with kitchen paper, to

dry it. Sprinkle the Porcini and Thyme Salt over the chicken skin. Leave for about 2 minutes.

Once the 2 minutes have passed, heat a frying pan to a gentle-medium heat and place the chicken in the pan, skin-side down. Don't move the chicken around, leave it there on a medium heat for a minute or so, until the skin is crisp. This will also protect the chicken breast meat on the other side of the skin, and the breast will cook in the heat. Turn the chicken over - it should be golden and crisp, and continue to cook on the other side, until cooked through thoroughly. Add a little mild, unflavoured coconut oil or avocado oil if you need to - the amount of oil in the pan will depend on how fatty your chicken breast skin is.

Cook the chicken breast thoroughly - about 5-7 minutes, depending on size. You can also remove the chicken to a baking tray if you prefer, and roast until cooked through. If you cut into it and any pink juices trickle out, cook it for a bit longer and check again. Once thoroughly cooked, lay the chicken breasts out on a clean board and slice. Serve straight away.

Lemon and Dill Smoked Mackerel Salad

We're always being told to add oily fish to our diets. They're rich in omega 3 oils, as well as calcium (if you eat the bones). I struggled with finding ways to eat mackerel for ages, until I found out about this salad. I absolutely love it, and it reminds me of clean, fresh Scandinavian dishes. The sharp lemon contrasts with the smoky, oily fish and the fresh dill lifts and gives the dish an uplifting, clean flavour. Healthy and ready in seconds, give this a try next time smoked mackerel is on your shopping list. Serves 1.

1-2 ready to eat smoked mackerel fillets (choose the ones without peppercorns)
juice of 1 lemon
a few sprigs of fresh dill
watercress, spinach and rocket leaves, to serve
2 tbsp extra virgin olive oil
1 teaspoonful of capers

Method
Take the mackerel fillets and gently peel off the skin, and flake the fish into a small bowl. Don't break the fish up into tiny pieces, keep them just about bite-sized. Cut a lemon in half and squeeze the juice over the mackerel. Pick the leaves off the dill springs and add them to the bowl, mixing well.

On a serving plate, arrange the watercress, rocket and spinach leaves and tip the mackerel mixture into the centre of the leaves. Drizzle any of the lemon juice left in the bowl around the leaves and finish with the olive oil, and scatter over a few capers. Eat straight away.

AIP Chinese-Style Lemon Chicken

When I posted this recipe up on the blog, I received comments from readers who couldn't wait to try it, to try and rekindle some of the memories of their favourite Chinese takeaways before AIP. When they did, I was so pleased that so many of them loved it. The recipe came about after I found an old notebook I used to scribble down ideas for recipes in. As I flicked through, I found an old recipe for Lemon Chicken, and had discovered it was basically lemon juice, stock, sugar and cornflour. And when I made this AIP-compliant version, it was perfect. It's not as sweet as I remember the takeaway version being, but more tangy. The tapioca starch gives the chicken a slight chewy coating and toasty flavour. It's one of my favourites, and you can make it in minutes. Serve with Chinese-Style Seaweed and some of your favourite vegetable noodles alongside. Serves 2.

juice of 1 lemon
200ml (7 fl. oz) chicken or vegetable stock or broth
2 heaped tablespoons runny honey
1 teaspoon coconut sugar
1 tbsp mild, unflavoured coconut oil
2 chicken breasts, sliced on the diagonal into medium-sized chunks
2 tbsp tapioca flour
1 large spring onion
1 tsp arrowroot powder, mixed with 1 tbsp cold water
pinch of salt

Method
First, make the sauce. Combine the lemon juice, chicken or vegetable broth or stock, honey and the coconut sugar in a small saucepan. Turn on the heat, stirring, and bring to a light simmer. Turn down the heat while you cook the chicken.

Measure the tapioca flour out into a wide, shallow bowl and toss the chicken slices in it, to coat. Heat the coconut oil in a frying pan and fry the tapioca-dusted chicken for a few minutes on each side, until cooked through and golden.

Once the chicken is just cooked and golden on the outside, quickly chop the spring onion and add it to the frying pan to soften with the cooked chicken (use a different board to the one you sliced the chicken on, or I usually just snip the spring onion into the pan using scissors).

Turn your attention now to the sauce, which will have reduced a little in the pan. Pour the arrowroot and water mixture into the sauce and stir until combined and slightly thickened. You can now either pour the sauce over the cooked chicken or serve the chicken and then drizzle the sauce over. Season with a small pinch of salt and serve hot.

Notes:
You can also grate the zest of the lemon into the sauce for a stronger flavour, if you like.
If you're alarmed by the honey and coconut sugar in the recipe, the honey is essential but the coconut sugar adds a slight toffee flavour and a deeper colour rather than further sweetness. You could have a go at omitting the coconut sugar but you'll end up with a lighter coloured sauce.

Lamb Do Piaza

Lamb Do Piaza is one of my favourite curries. I love its richness, the thick aromatic sauce and tender lamb that melts under your fork. This curry is quite onion-rich, and here you have the onions blended into the sauce as well as the fried onions on top. The sauce feels like a tomato-based sauce, but there are no nightshades. If you're missing curry night on AIP, definitely try this one. You'll love it. Oh, and this curry is lovely with my AIP Naan Breads on the side. Serves 4.

2 tsp preferred cooking fat
500g (1lb) diced lamb shoulder
3 cloves of garlic, peeled and chopped
2 white onions, peeled (one onion chopped, the other one sliced)
thick slice of ginger (about 2cm (half an inch) thick)

1 carrot, peeled and chopped
pinch of cloves
pinch of cinnamon
1 tsp turmeric
300ml (1 and a quarter cups) beef or lamb broth or stock
1 small cooked beetroot, skin removed
salt, if needed, to taste

Method

Heat 1 tsp of the cooking fat or oil in a large frying pan and fry the lamb until golden and browned on the outside. Lift out and place in the bottom of the dish of your slow cooker. You should still have some fat left in the pan. Fry the garlic for a few seconds until aromatic and then add the chopped onion, leaving the sliced onion for later. Add the chopped ginger, carrot, cloves, cinnamon, turmeric and fry for a minute.

Pour in the stock or broth and quickly chop up the cooked beetroot, adding this to the pan to warm through. Continue to simmer for 10-15 minutes, or until the vegetables are tender and the sauce is aromatic.

Once the carrots are soft, carefully blend the sauce until smooth - it'll be hot (I use a stick blender) and then pour into your slow cooker dish, stirring the lamb into the sauce. Put on the lid and leave to cook on high for 4 hours, until the lamb is tender.

Once the lamb is cooked through and tender and can be squished with a fork, quickly melt the remaining 1 tsp fat or oil in a clean frying pan and fry the sliced onion until golden. Turn off the heat and serve the curry with the fried onion slices on top and some fresh coriander/cilantro leaves. Season with salt if you think it needs it.

Creamy Spinach and Chicken Curry

I always love spinach in my Indian recipes. It gives such an earthy flavour and tinges the sauce a nice shade of green. I love using frozen spinach, because it's convenient (no washing or chopping) and it comes in little icy blocks - you just drop a couple into your favourite dishes. Frozen spinach also seems to have a much more concentrated flavour than fresh leaves. You might notice that the sauce in the photo has separated slightly from the creamy coconut milk. This is down to the moisture from the spinach leaves. Just give it a stir and it's perfect again. Serves 4.

1 tsp preferred cooking fat
1 small onion, peeled and chopped
2 spring onions, washed, trimmed and chopped
1 x 400ml (14 fl.oz.) can full fat coconut milk
2-3 small blocks of frozen spinach
2 x skinless and boneless chicken breasts, chopped into bite-sized chunks
pinch of cloves
half teaspoon ground ginger
1 tsp turmeric
salt, to taste

Method
Melt the cooking fat or oil in a medium-sized saucepan and fry the garlic cloves and onion for a minute until sizzling and aromatic. Pour in the coconut milk and add the spinach, chicken

breast pieces, the pinch of cloves, ginger and the turmeric. Leave everything to bubble gently, with the lid off, for 20 minutes or so, until the chicken is cooked through and the sauce is sweet, mild and fragrant. Give it a stir and serve straight away.

AIP Red Thai Vegetable Curry

When I made (and quickly devoured) my AIP Green Thai Curry recipe I knew I needed a Red Thai Curry equivalent. So I made one. The great thing is that this paste, when it's fried until fragrant and then stirred with coconut milk, tastes pretty authentic. The only thing you don't get is the heat, because there are no chillies on AIP, but you could add some fresh ginger or horseradish root to up the heat if you wanted to. It's a beautiful orange-pink colour, and while the green paste is all zesty and citrussy,  *this one is sweeter. It makes a wonderful change. I've used vegetables in this curry, but you could add sliced beef, chicken, seafood, fish or turkey. And don't be put off by the long list of ingredients - most of it is chucked in a food processor and whizzed into a paste in seconds. Serves 4.*

2 sticks of lemongrass
2 cloves of garlic
bunch of fresh coriander/cilantro leaves
bunch of fresh basil leaves

juice of half a lime
1 tsp worth of freshly grated or chopped ginger
a quarter of a teaspoon fish sauce
1 small cooked beetroot
1 tsp preferred cooking fat
400ml (14 fl.oz) can full fat coconut milk
quarter tsp ground turmeric
2 spring onions, washed, trimmed and chopped
100g (3.5 oz) cauliflower florets
2 carrots, peeled and cut into ribbons
salt to taste
lime juice and coriander leaves to serve

Method
First, make the paste. Quickly trim and pull off the outer layer from the lemongrass and then chop roughly into chunks. Peel the cloves of garlic. Add the lemongrass and garlic to a food processor along with the stalks from the bunch of coriander/cilantro (save the leaves for later), the basil (stalks and leaves), lime juice, ginger, fish sauce and beetroot. Pulse in the processor until it all forms a coarse but well-blended paste.

Melt the cooking fat or oil in a large saucepan or frying pan and stir in the curry paste. Stir-fry until sizzling and aromatic, for about 3-4 minutes. Tip in the coconut milk and add the turmeric. Drop in the vegetables and simmer for about 10-15 minutes, or until the vegetables are cooked and tender. Taste, adding a little salt if you think it needs it, and serve in bowls with lime wedges for squeezing over and fresh coriander/cilantro leaves scattered on top.

Roasted Salmon and Parsnips with Dill Gremolata

Gremolata is a mixture of chopped parsley, garlic and lemon zest that's spooned over grilled meats and fish. And I decided I would make a version that also included dill and spoon it over cooked salmon. It was gorgeous. Hope you love it. Serves 4.

1 tbsp preferred cooking fat (mild, unflavoured coconut oil or lard
4 large parsnips, peeled and cut into bite-sized chunks
large sprig of fresh dill
half side of salmon, boneless if you can get it, but with the skin on, preferably
pinch of salt
1 lemon
small bunch of parsley
1 garlic clove
3 spring (green) onions, trimmed and chopped

Method
First, melt the fat in a roasting dish and slide into an oven preheated to 200°C/gas mark 6/400°F. After a minute, take it out and add the parsnip chunks, stirring it gently so they're all coated in the fat. Tear off some of the fresh dill leaves and stir these into the parsnips, along with a pinch of salt. Place it back in the oven to roast for 20 minutes.

After the 20 minutes are up, and the parsnips have had a good head-start on cooking, take the half side of salmon and lay it gently over the parsnips. Return to the oven for another 20 minutes, or until the parsnips are cooked through and tender and the salmon is cooked thoroughly. If it needs a bit more time, put it back in the oven for a few more minutes.

While the salmon and parsnips are cooking, make the gremolata. Chop the parsley and the rest of the dill and place in a bowl. Add the grated zest of the lemon and peel and chop the garlic clove. Stir everything together and put to one side.

Once the salmon and parsnips are cooked, take the dish out of the oven and throw in the chopped spring onions. They should start to wilt and soften in the heat of the other ingredients. If you want them cooked a bit more, just sprinkle them in in the last 5 minutes or so of cooking.

Serve the salmon with the dill gremolata spooned over and the roasted parsnips and spring onions underneath.

Scallops with Saffron and Orange Sauce

I became fascinated with how lemon juice paired so well with seafood - and then I realised that it wasn't just lemon juice that worked - orange and lime juice pepped it up as well. I decided to play around and add saffron to the mix. It's a main component of Spanish paella, which combines rice, seafood and chicken - so why wouldn't it work? It did. This is a beautiful, earthily fragrant dish for a light lunch served with vegetables on the side, or for a special occasion. Serves 2.

juice of 1 large orange
small pinch of saffron strands
pinch of salt
1 tsp coconut cream
1 tsp preferred cooking fat (I use mild unflavoured coconut oil)
8-10 fresh scallops
Freshly chopped parsley - about 1 tbsp, to serve

Method
Mix together the orange juice, saffron strands and salt in a small saucepan and put on a low heat, stirring often. As the sauce starts

bubbling, add the teaspoonful of coconut cream to thicken and give richness to the sauce and turn off the heat.

In a small frying pan, heat the coconut oil on a medium heat and gently place the scallops in. Start at the top of the pan (where the number 12 would be on a clock) and place them evenly around the pan in a circle. Fry on one side for about 3 minutes and then, starting back at the "12" position in pan, turn them over one by one and fry on the other side for another 2 minutes or so, until cooked thoroughly but not overcooked.

Divide the warm sauce between two plates and place the scallops on top. Sprinkle with the freshly chopped parsley.

Smoky, Sweet, Herby Pork Ribs

Who doesn't love meltingly tender pork ribs, all crispened up and caramelised under the grill? I do. And I became determined to develop a pork rib marinade that would hit the spot. I cook these in the slow cooker, and the meat really does just fall off the bone. All it then needs is a quick blast under the heat of the grill and they're ready. Serves 3-4.

4-5 meaty pork spare ribs, on the bone
1 tsp coconut sugar
1 tsp dried thyme
half teaspoon dried basil
half teaspoon smoked sea salt
quarter teaspoon onion powder
1 tbsp honey

Method
First, preheat your slow cooker to high. In a small bowl, mix the coconut sugar, thyme, basil, smoked sea salt and onion powder. Place the spare ribs on a board or plate and rub them all over with

the spices, making sure it's all completely covered. Clatter the ribs into the pot of your slow cooker and replace the lid (you don't need to add any liquid) and leave to cook for 4-5 hours, until a poke with a fork reveals they're tender and cooked through.

Next, line a baking tray or grill pan with foil and, using tongs, arrange the hot slow cooked ribs in one layer on it. Drizzle with the honey and then slide under the grill for 3-4 minutes before turning over and grilling the other side. You could also do this bit on a barbecue, if you like. Once the ribs are slightly golden and sizzling serve them while they're still hot. Any leftovers can be shredded off the bone, refrigerated and flaked into salads.

Sides

We often tend to think about the main element of our food first - what meat or fish we're serving and what will work well with it. But there's so much fun to be had with side dishes, too. You can play with spices in breads, side salads or veggies - there are some Indian-inspired recipes here, as well as others using herbs you might not have thought of.

Discovering the AIP Naan Breads was a big step in me enjoying AIP curry night. It meant I could dip them into the sauce, and use them to scoop out the curry, just as you do when eating a Balti. The naan really does have a dense, chewy texture, so they stand up to a bit of dipping.

Let your side dishes take centre stage while you have fun with these recipes.

Coriander and Garlic Naan Breads

If you've ever wished for something dense and bread-like to serve alongside an aromatic curry or stew, then here's the answer: AIP-compliant naan breads flavoured with garlic and fresh coriander leaves. It tastes great, and is chewy and dense in texture, standing up well for dipping. Makes 5-6 naan breads.

2 medium green plantains (they must be green), peeled
quarter teaspoon of garlic salt (or garlic powder and a small pinch of salt)
1 tbsp mild, unflavoured coconut oil, or avocado oil
Pinch of nutritional yeast
1 tbsp finely chopped fresh coriander/cilantro leaves

Method
Chop the peeled plantains into small chunks and add to a blender with the garlic salt, oil and nutritional yeast. Blend until smooth. you'll be left with a very thick, pale batter. Stir in the chopped coriander/ cilantro leaves.

Line a baking tray with a piece of greaseproof paper and grease slightly with coconut oil. Drop heaped tablespoon-fuls of the batter on the baking tray and smooth into a rough-looking circle or oval shape, so that each circle of dough is about half a centimetre thick.

Bake for 15 minutes at gas mark 6/200°C/400°F, turning over half way through cooking. They should look slightly golden in colour and have a firm texture. The naan breads are best eaten warm, just after they come out of the oven.

Roasted Squash with Rosemary and Honey

For this recipe I used a small white pumpkin-like squash, although you could use any variety. The sweet flesh caramelises in the heat of the oven and the rosemary leaves add depth and an aromatic, slightly sweet-aniseed flavour. This is especially good alongside a freshly roasted chicken. Lovely. Serves 2-3.

1 small white squash, about 500g (1lb)
melted mild unflavoured coconut oil or avocado oil
a few fresh rosemary sprigs

pinch of salt
1 tbsp runny honey

Method
Carefully slice the squash along its equator, removing the seeds and stringy parts of the flesh as you go. Arrange the squash slices in a shallow roasting tray, in one layer. Pull the pine-like leaves off the stems and scatter them all over the squash along with a pinch of salt.

Roast at gas mark 7/220ºC/ 425ºF for about 15-20 minutes, until tender and slightly golden and then drizzle with a little honey before serving.

Raw Carrot Salad with Ginger and Lime Dressing

This is a crunchy salad that you can eat with pretty much anything. The tanginess of the ginger and lime contrasts well with the sweetness of the raw carrots. Serves 2-3.

2 large carrots, spiralized on a thin setting, cut into strips with a julienne peeler, or coarsely grated
1cm slice of fresh ginger, peeled and finely grated
juice of 1 lime
1 tbsp extra virgin olive oil
pinch of salt
2 tbsp freshly chopped coriander/cilantro leaves, to serve

Method
Put the spiralized carrots in a serving bowl.

Mix the grated ginger, lime juice, olive oil and salt together and pour over the carrots, tossing well to coat. Scatter with freshly chopped coriander/cilantro leaves and serve straight away. This salad is best eaten on the day it's made, but leftovers will keep for a day, covered in the fridge.

Sweet Potato and Chive Mash

One of my favourite sides; soft, velvety sweet potatoes are mashed and bacon fat is added (stir in the cooked, chopped bacon pieces too, if you like) along with snipped chives. Perfect. Serves 4.

3 large orange-fleshed sweet potatoes
scant 1 tsp bacon fat (or just chop 3 smoked streaky bacon rashers and dry-fry them in a pan until the fat renders down. Save the bacon for later, or stir them into the mash to finish, if you like).
Sea salt
small handful of chives

Method
Peel and roughly chop the sweet potatoes into one inch pieces and put them in a saucepan. Just cover them with cold water, and bring to a gentle boil on a medium heat. The sweet potatoes should take around 10 minutes to cook and turn completely

tender. Check they're cooked with the tip of a sharp knife and then drain thoroughly, leaving in the colander on the draining board for the moment.

Melt the bacon fat in the saucepan until sizzling and then tumble in the sweet potatoes, turning off the heat. Mash them well, until they're smooth and silky and add a pinch or two of salt. Give the chives a rinse and then, using scissors, snip them into small pieces and fold them into the mash. Beat the mash until smooth and fluffy and serve straight away.

Quick Balsamic Caramelised Onions

Caramelised onions are one of my favourite side dishes. I often make a batch when we have a barbecue, to serve alongside burgers and meats. The only thing is that usually you have to cook the onion long and slow to start the caramelisation process. I was making them one day when I realised that balsamic vinegar has many of the same deep, rich flavours as the onion has when cooked for a long time - so it might help speed up the process. It does.

1 large red onion
1 tbsp lard or mild, flavourless coconut oil
1 tbsp coconut sugar

splash of balsamic vinegar
pinch of salt

Method
Peel the onion and slice very thinly. Melt the oil or lard in a frying pan and add the onion, frying gently until softened and beginning to take on a bit of golden colour. Stir in the coconut sugar, the balsamic vinegar and salt, and continue to cook, until the onions have darkened and wilted down. They should be soft and jammy. Transfer to a serving bowl and serve just warm or cooled.

Salted Plantain Fries with Garlic and Parsley

Green plantains are a good substitute for potatoes in many ways. One of my favourite ways to eat them is like this - made into fries. They were inspired by a portion of fries I ate at a restaurant once. They came to my table, still sizzling from the fryer, and scattered with garlic and freshly-chopped parsley. I ate them years ago and still think about them, they were so good. These fries only take around 20 minutes to cook. Serves 2-3.

2 green plantains, peeled
3 tbsp avocado oil or flavourless mild coconut oil
1 large clove of garlic, peeled and finely chopped
small handful finely chopped fresh parsley
pinch of sea salt

Method
Put the peeled plantains on a chopping board, and with a sharp knife, cut them into sticks.

Get out a baking sheet and line with greaseproof paper. Drizzle in the oil and add the plantain fries, tossing them to make sure they're all coated. Slide into the oven and roast at gas mark 7/210°C/425°F for 10-15 minutes, until sizzling and tender. Once they're cooked through, take them out of the oven and immediately scatter them with the garlic, parsley and a pinch of salt. Give them a shake and serve. The garlic and parsley will wilt slightly and soften in the heat of the fries.

Spaghetti Squash with Bacon and Crispy Sage

Spaghetti squash is a recent discovery of mine - I've only just been able to get it in our local supermarket, so when it's available I grab a couple and cook them in advance, scoop out the insides and then keep it in a bowl in the fridge for quick stir-fries. Spaghetti squash has a mild, sweet flavour and it contrasts really well here with the salty, smoky bacon and the crisp, earthy sage leaves. Serves 4.

1 medium-sized spaghetti squash
3 rashers of smoked, streaky bacon
small handful of fresh sage leaves (about 5 leaves)
pinch or two of salt

Method
First, cook the spaghetti squash. Preheat your oven to gas mark 6/200°C/400°F and get out a deep roasting tray or ovenproof dish.

Place the spaghetti squash carefully on a board and slice it in half around its equator - not down towards the stalk. This will ensure that the spaghetti-like strands will be longer and easier to twirl around your fork. Place the squash halves cut side down in the roasting dish and pour in enough cold water to come half way up the squash halves. Roast for about 35 minutes, until the squash flesh is tender and can be easily scraped with a fork. The time the squash takes to cook will depend on its size, so if you need to put it back in an extra few minutes, do so and just check on it again.

Once the spaghetti squash is tender, take it out of the oven and let it cool. Flip the cooled squash cut side up and place on a board. You can now scrape the flesh with a fork, starting at the outer edges of the cut squash, letting it come away in strands. Scoop these up with a spoon and place them in a bowl. At this point you can let the squash fully cool (it's usually still warm in the middle) and then cover with cling film and keep in the fridge for 2-3 days, taking out a handful as and when you need it.

To make the squash with bacon and crispy sage, cut the bacon into small pieces and dry-fry in a pan until golden and crisp. Remove from the pan with a slotted spoon, keeping the bacon fat in the pan. Wash and dry the sage leaves and lay them carefully into the pan - cook them for a minute on each side, and you should see them start to crisp up and turn dark. Lift the crispy sage leaves out and add them to the bacon. Next, add a little mild, unflavoured coconut or avocado oil if you need it, and fry a couple of handfuls of the cooked, cooled spaghetti squash strands for 2-3 minutes, until hot. Add the bacon pieces and the sage and stir-fry, mixing all the ingredients well. Allow the leaves to break up in the pan as you toss and stir the other ingredients together. Season to taste with a pinch of salt and serve straight away.

Chinese Takeout Style Seaweed

Believe me when I say that this recipe makes great-tasting, authentic Chinese takeaway 'seaweed'. We all know it's not actually seaweed and it's just deep-fried cabbage, but I love the crunch and the way the flavour of the greens changes after cooking and becomes sweeter. I tried this recipe a few times with cabbage, but it just never reached the consistency I wanted. I tried it with kale and it worked. Incredibly well. Make this for your next home-made takeout. I like the leaves quite chunky, but if you're after an authentic takeaway-style result, chop them very finely before frying. Serves 2.

1 tsp mild, unflavoured coconut oil
100g (3.5 oz) curly kale leaves, tough stalks removed, chopped quite finely
pinch of sea salt
half teaspoon coconut sugar

Method
Stir-fry the chopped kale (the finer you chop it the better the texture will be in the finished result) in the coconut oil until just crisp and slightly golden. Turn off the heat and stir in the salt and sugar. Or, for a more authentic takeaway finish, stir in the salt and half the sugar and then take to the table with the remaining quarter teaspoon of sugar sprinkled over the top. Serve straight away.

Beetroot Salad with Garlic and Parsley

I've come to the conclusion that (on savoury grounds, obviously) there's not much that you can't eat with a garlic and parsley chimichurri-style dressing. I've seen beetroot served with dressing like this as tapas dishes. The fresh parsley adds fragrance to the sweet beetroot and the garlic adds a spicy pungency. The whole thing is pulled together by the vinegar and oil. We make this quite often when we have a barbecue. It's colourful and tasty alongside grilled meats and fish. Serves 3-4, as a side salad.

3 small beetroots, cooked, trimmed and peeled and left to cool (you can use the shop-bought cooked beets to save time, just don't use the ones in vinegar)
1 chunky garlic clove
small handful fresh parsley
1 tsp sherry vinegar (or use apple cider vinegar if you prefer)
1 tbsp extra virgin olive oil

Method
Chop up the beetroot into chunky bite-sized wedges. Roughly chop the garlic and the parsley and throw it into a bowl with the beetroot chunks. Stir in the sherry vinegar and the olive oil and stir to mix. You can add a pinch of salt, if you like too - check for seasoning and then serve.

Artichoke Salad with Chives and Garlic

I use canned artichoke hearts for this recipe, which is beautiful alongside grilled meats, especially lamb. There's a little bit of heat from the fresh garlic but rather than the citrussy parsley, I've added snipped chives for a mild onion-like flavour. Serves 4, as a side dish or side salad.

400g (14 oz) can of cooked artichoke hearts, drained
1 clove of garlic, peeled and finely chopped
small handful of chives, snipped into small pieces
2-3 tbsp extra virgin olive oil

Method
Combine the drained artichoke hearts, the chopped garlic, chives and olive oil into a bowl and stir well. Serve cold, alongside grilled and roasted meats and fish. It's especially good with grilled lamb.

BBQ Sweet Potato Fries

Nightshade spices like paprika and chilli often form a big part of BBQ style spice blends. Here's a nightshade-free AIP version with just a few ingredients. Next time you make sweet potato fries, give this recipe a try. We love it. Oh, and we leave the skin on - they give an incredible amount of extra flavour as well as help stop them breaking up in the roasting tray. Serves 4.

2 tsp coconut sugar
half teaspoon dried thyme
quarter teaspoon smoked sea salt
2 large sweet potatoes
mild, unflavoured coconut oil

Method
First, mix together the coconut sugar, dried thyme and the smoked sea salt and put to one side.

Peel the sweet potatoes (or leave the skin on, if you like) and cut them into fries. Put the coconut oil on a large, shallow baking tray and slide into an oven preheated to gas mark 7/220°C/425°F for a few seconds to melt. Take the tray back out of the oven and arrange the sweet potato fries in one layer. Sprinkle over the BBQ seasoning and toss to coat the sweet potato chips well. Slide the tray back into the oven and cook for 25 minutes, giving the tray a shake about half-way through cooking, until the fries are tender, golden and slightly crisp.

Roasted Balsamic Mushrooms with Thyme

I know people who say they don't like mushrooms, but fall in love with them when they're roasted. Roasting mushrooms brings out their natural savoury flavours, enhancing them. I roast mine with fresh thyme sprigs, to help lift the flavour and add fragrance.

Adding the balsamic vinegar gives the mushrooms a deep, sweet flavour. Serves 2-3.

200g (7oz) mushrooms (I used brown chestnut mushrooms)
quarter teaspoon of garlic salt or garlic powder
1 tbsp balsamic vinegar
a few sprigs of fresh thyme
1 tbsp avocado oil or olive oil

Method
Clean the mushrooms and trim the stalks if necessary, and arrange them on a roasting tray. Season with the garlic salt or powder and drizzle over the balsamic vinegar. Strew the thyme sprigs over and drizzle with the oil. Roast at gas mark 6/200°C/ 400°F for about 20 minutes, or until the mushrooms are sizzling and slightly golden.

Bacon and Rosemary Hasselback Sweet Potatoes

These are the business. I love them. As well as being a pretty good side dish, they're perfect as a meal in their own right - an alternative to a baked sweet potato. There's all sorts going on here - sweet, salty, soft, crunchy - and then you get all the aniseed-sweetness from the rosemary. Serves 2.

2 medium-sized orange-fleshed sweet potatoes
3 rashers of streaky bacon (and some mild, unflavoured coconut oil, if necessary)
1 tsp dried rosemary (or use fresh if you have it)

Method

First, wash the sweet potatoes, dry them with a tea towel and then place them on a chopping board. With a sharp knife, cut little slits in the sweet potato, about half a centimetre apart, but don't cut all the way through. Place the sweet potatoes in an ovenproof baking tray or roasting tin.

Snip the bacon into small pieces, using scissors, and drop them into a frying pan. Gently fry the bacon pieces so they render down their fat, for 2-3 minutes. If your bacon doesn't have enough fat then feel free to add a teaspoonful of mild, unflavoured coconut oil to help it along. You want to have a teaspoon or two of bacony fat or oil in the pan. Remove the bacon when it's cooked, with a slotted spoon, and then lift it out of the pan and into a saucer or small bowl, leaving the oil in the frying pan.

Throw the rosemary into the hot oil or fat and let it sizzle for a second or two. Lift the pan and trickle the oil all over the sweet potatoes, trying to get the fat and the rosemary in between the slits you just cut. Leave the bacon to one side for the moment and slide the tray into an oven preheated to 200C/gas mark 6. Roast for 40 minutes, until the sweet potato is cooked through and tender.

Serve the sweet potatoes with the bacon sprinkled all over the top. You can slide the bacon-strewn potatoes back in the oven if you like, for a minute or two, to reheat the bacon.

Parsnip Saag Aloo

Saag Aloo was always one of the side dishes that I ordered when I went out for curry in my pre-AIP days. It's a dry-ish curry of potato and spinach. I never found it particularly spicy, it was generally fairly mild - but it was a tasty dish to have on the table.

When I found out that AIP didn't allow potatoes in the initial elimination stage I searched for the most satisfying alternative. I've tried lots of different vegetables but I think parsnips are one of the best. You could also adapt this recipe to include white sweet potatoes or possibly even green plantains, although I haven't tried it. Serves 4.

1 tsp preferred cooking fat or oil
2 medium-sized parsnips (about one and a half cups worth), peeled and chopped into large chunks
1 large clove of garlic, peeled and chopped
1 tsp freshly grated ginger
pinch of salt
pinch of ground cloves
1 tsp turmeric
150g leaf spinach (I use frozen)

Method
Heat the fat or oil in a medium-sized lidded frying pan and add the parsnip chunks. Fry them until just sizzling, and then add the garlic, ginger, salt, ground cloves, turmeric and leaf spinach. Add a small splash of water and then put the lid on and simmer gently until the parsnips are tender and everything is heated through, about 10-15 minutes.

Roasted Sweet Potato and Red Onion with Black Garlic

If you've never tried black (or fermented) garlic, I urge you to get hold of some and try it. It brings a completely new, sticky-sweet flavour to sweet and savoury foods. When combined with roasted sweet potatoes and red onion it has a deeply rich, sweet, balsamic flavour. Sprinkle with a little parsley to lift all those sweet flavours and you have a beautiful side dish that will get people talking. Serves 3-4.

1 tsp preferred cooking oil or fat
2 medium sized sweet potatoes, peeled and chopped into small, bite-sized chunks
1 red onion, peeled and chopped
3 cloves of black garlic, eased from their papery skins and chopped
1 tbsp freshly chopped parsley
2 tbsp extra virgin olive oil
salt, to taste

Method
Get out a shallow roasting dish and spoon in the cooking fat. Preheat your oven to gas mark 6/200ºC/400ºF and slide the dish into the oven for a minute or so, until the fat melts.

Using oven gloves, side the dish out of the oven and add the chopped sweet potatoes. Stir them with a spoon, so they're evenly coated in the fat, and then put them back into the oven and cook for 15 minutes.

After the 15 minutes is up, take the dish out of the oven (using oven gloves - it'll be hot) and then sprinkle in the chopped onion. Give it all a stir and return to the oven for another 10 minutes, or until the sweet potatoes are gently roasted and tender when pierced with a fork.

Once the sweet potatoes are cooked, quickly whisk together the olive oil, chopped black garlic cloves and parsley and pour this mixture all over the roasted sweet potatoes and onion. Give it a good stir to coat thoroughly and season with a little salt if you think it needs it. Serve straight away.

Indian-Style Mushroom Cauliflower Rice

Here's an Indian-style cauliflower rice dish that's mildly spiced and includes mushrooms. It's based on one of our favourite takeaway side dishes and will work brilliantly alongside grilled or roasted meats or any one of the Indian-style curries in this book. The cauliflower is fried with the spices and ends up with quite a nutty flavour. Serves 3-4.

1 tsp preferred cooking fat
200g mushrooms (about 7 oz) (I use brown, 'chestnut' mushrooms), cleaned, trimmed and sliced
1 clove of garlic, peeled and chopped
1 small onion, peeled and chopped
half teaspoon freshly grated ginger
1 tsp ground turmeric
small pinch of ground cloves
2 cups cauliflower florets, whizzed in a food processor for a few seconds to make grain-like 'rice'
salt, to taste
small handful of freshly chopped coriander leaf/cilantro

Method
Heat the fat in a large frying pan and add the mushrooms. Stir-fry until golden and well-cooked. Most of the moisture will have leaked out of the mushrooms and then dried up again. This will give a more intense flavour.

Next, stir in the garlic, onion, ginger, turmeric and ground cloves and fry until aromatic - about 1 minute. Tumble in the cauliflower 'rice' and then stir-fry so that the cauliflower gets coated in the spices and aromatics. Add a splash of water and season with a little salt. Continue to cook, stirring, until the cauliflower is tender. This will only take about 3-4 minutes.

Once the cauliflower rice is cooked to your liking, turn off the heat and scatter in the chopped coriander leaf/cilantro. Stir it together and serve while hot.

Grilled Courgettes with Basil Oil

Courgettes cook really quickly and when grilled under direct heat, have a toasty nuttiness to them as the surface browns slightly. This is a really quick side dish that you can make in just a few minutes, inspired by a dish I was once served at a fish restaurant in Christchurch, on the south coast of the UK. Courgettes and the sweet, aromatic scent of the Basil Oil work so well together - it's now one of my favourite combinations. Serves 2, as a side dish.

2 medium sized courgettes/zucchini
1 tbsp extra virgin olive oil or avocado oil
pinch of salt
juice of 1 lemon
Basil Oil, to serve

Method
Wash and trim the courgettes/zucchini and slice on the diagonal. Place in a bowl and trickle over the olive oil, sprinkle on the salt and squeeze in the lemon juice. Toss with your hands to coat the courgettes well in the mixture and then arrange the slices in one single layer on a grill tray.

Slide under the grill and cook for 4-5 minutes, until they soften and turn slightly golden. Slide them back out and carefully, using tongs, turn them over and cook on the other side. Keep an eye on them, making sure they don't burn.

Once they're cooked, arrange the courgette/zucchini slices on a serving plate and drizzle the basil oil over the top. Serve straight away.

Roasted Parsnips with Rosemary and Garlic

Since I realised that parsnips were my favourite potato substitute, I've been trying out my old favourite potato recipes using them. And this one was a big hit. The parsnips turn golden and sweeten in the oven, as the roast in the fragrant garlic and fresh rosemary. If you can't get hold of fresh rosemary sprigs, used dried. Serves 4.

500g (1lb) parsnips, peeled and chopped into bite-sized chunks
5 cloves of garlic, unpeeled
2 sprigs of fresh rosemary, washed
pinch of salt
1 tbsp avocado or olive oil - or your preferred cooking fat

Method
Add the parsnip chunks to an oven-proof roasting tray or dish, along with the garlic cloves and rosemary sprigs. Season with salt and drizzle over the oil, and slide into an oven preheated to gas mark 6/200°C/400°F. Roast for 25-30 minutes, or until tender and golden.

Drinks and Sweet Treats

A few years ago, I lived by dessert. I'd eat lunch and need a sweet treat afterwards. I'd finish dinner and reach for the ice cream tub. I'd buy handfuls of chocolate bars to eat as a snack. There were a few times I even ate trifle for breakfast. Nowadays, I have a different kind of respect for sweet treats. They're good for just that - a treat - but even if the ingredients are all AIP compliant, it doesn't mean you have the go ahead to eat it all day, every day. Natural sugars like honey and maple syrup are still sugar after all, and I find they can still set off cravings. So now, when I do treat myself to a dessert I eat it slowly and mindfully, enjoying all the flavours and textures.

Here, I've introduced a range of spices and herbs into drinks and desserts. Mint leaves in drinks, warm chai tea flavours in ice lollies and a tea cake. And if you've never tasted basil and strawberries together, go try it now. Instead of tasting like basil or strawberries it tastes like the most tropical, fragrant pineapple you've ever tasted. This is where I love to have fun with flavours. Sometimes when they're paired up, they taste nothing like each other but end up creating a brand new flavour altogether.

Mint Mojito
This is such a refreshing drink to serve on a hot day, or just when you need to lift your spirits - it's refreshing and alcohol-free. Makes 1.

4 ice cubes
small sprig of fresh mint leaves
juice of 1 lime
plain, chilled sparkling water - about 150ml

Drop the ice cubes into a glass and push in the mint leaves. Squeeze in the juice of a lime and add a couple of slices if you like to the glass for extra citrus flavour. Top up with sparkling water and push down the mint with a spoon or straw, to get the oils infused into the drink.

Pomegranate Fizz

This drink is really simple to make. The combination of sweet-sour and sticky pomegranate molasses, with fresh pomegranate juice and sparkling water makes this a fizzy, fruity party drink for a special celebration. Pomegranate molasses is incredibly tart and very sweet at the same time, so it's also good for adding to salad dressings. Makes 2 glasses.

approx 300ml (one and a quarter cups) plain, sparkling water
2 tsp pomegranate molasses
1 fresh pomegranate

Method
Take two glasses and fill each one with the sparkling water. Stir a teaspoon of pomegranate molasses into each and stir in. Cut the pomegranate in half and squeeze the juice out of each half and into the glasses. Taste, and add more pomegranate juice if you think it needs more fruitiness.

Warm Chai Tea

I absolutely love chai tea. You need a strong, black tea for the base - use whatever black tea bags you have, the stronger the better. I use Assam tea bags, which is a strong blend of black tea. It's my favourite treat to snuggle up with after a long day. Makes 1 mug.

1 Assam (or strong black tea), tea bag
1 whole clove
quarter teaspoon vanilla extract
1 tsp coconut sugar
5cm long cinnamon stick
300ml (1 and a quarter cups) boiling water, from the kettle
full-fat coconut milk, to taste

Method
Place the tea bag, clove, vanilla extract, coconut sugar and cinnamon stick in a medium-sized jug and then pour over the boiling water. Allow everything to steep together for 4-5 minutes and then strain the liquid into a mug, discarding the tea bag, clove and cinnamon stick. Add a drop of coconut milk. For a frothy texture, whisk vigorously or pour back into the jug and blitz with a stick blender.

Honey Swirl Cinnamon Ice Cream

I love figs. And I roasted them in my first ebook, Simple AIP Paleo Comfort Food. *Roasting them in a hot oven for about 10 minutes brings out their perfumed sweetness. Figs are a good source of magnesium and calcium too, so as well as being indulgent and flavoursome they're also pretty good for you. I love to serve them with this cinnamon ice cream flavoured with a honey swirl. The honey doesn't actually set in the freezer - it stays kind of sticky and luxurious. This ice cream is also wonderful served with any roasted fruits, especially apples, pears and berries. It makes me think of the flavours of Egypt - honey, figs, cinnamon - all luxurious, fragrant and sweet. Serves 6-8.*

400ml (14 fl oz) full fat
coconut milk
1 tsp ground cinnamon
1 tsp vanilla extract (heat first
to get rid of the alcohol, or use
vanilla powder if you can find
it)
2 tsp coconut sugar
a pinch of sea salt
2 tablespoons of honey

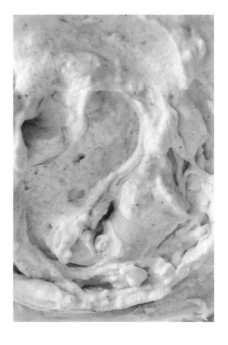

Method
In a bowl, mix together the
coconut milk, vanilla extract or
powder, coconut sugar and salt.
Cover and chill for a few
hours, preferably overnight.

When you're read to make the ice cream, pour the chilled mixture into the frozen bowl of an ice cream maker and churn for about 25 minutes until it's the consistency of soft-scoop ice cream. Scrape the ice cream into a freezer-proof tub and trickle over the honey, swirling it in the ice cream as you go. Replace the lid and freeze until ready to eat. Leave the ice cream at room temperature for a few minutes before serving, so it softens slightly.

Chai Tea Ice Lollies

Drinking a hot cup of chai tea is one thing, but when you go for a chai-spiced ice lolly it's a bit confusing at first. I like the way the warm spices and the ice-cold cream plays with your mind a bit. And they're as good in the winter months as they are in the summer. Makes 6 small lollies.

400ml (14 fl. oz) full fat coconut milk
1 cinnamon stick
6 whole cloves
2 tsp coconut sugar
2 Assam (or strong, plain black) tea bags
half a teaspoon vanilla extract

Method
Pour the coconut milk into a small saucepan and add the rest of the ingredients. Heat gently to a simmer and squish the tea bags against the side of the saucepan with tongs or a long spoon. You should end up with a warm, creamy caramel-coloured mixture. Turn off the heat. Strain the liquid so the whole spices and tea bags are discarded, and pour the liquid into lolly moulds. Freeze until set.

Coconut Butter Cinnamon Stuffed Dates

You can add a little spice to your kitchen worktop snack - pitted dates filled with coconut manna and cinnamon. Coconut manna is puréed coconut - it's sweet and silky, the coconut's equivalent of peanut butter - it's also called coconut butter. Ready in about 30 seconds. Go! Makes 6.

6 dates, pitted
3 tsp coconut manna or
coconut butter
pinch or two of ground
cinnamon

Method
Arrange the pitted dates out on
a board or plate and push about
half a teaspoon of coconut
manna or coconut butter into
the centre. Sprinkle over the
ground cinnamon and you're
done.

Raw Chai Tea Cake with Salted Caramel Chai Tea Frosting

I love this recipe. If I need to make a cake for a special occasion, I make this. There's no baking involved, which is a bonus, and it doesn't take long to put everything together. Just for treats, this cake is frosted with coconut cream and a date-based caramel sauce infused with the warm, cosy flavours of chai tea. Cuts into 8-10 squares.

100g (3.5oz) desiccated coconut
2 strong black tea bags
1 x 5cm long cinnamon stick
2 cloves
half teaspoon vanilla extract
good pinch of ground ginger
250g (9oz) pack of dates, pit removed
150ml (2/3 cup) coconut cream

Method
To make the cake, tip the coconut into a food processor and then boil the kettle.

Take the tea bags and drop them into a glass jug. Pour over 350ml boiling water and drop in the cinnamon, cloves, the vanilla extract and the ginger. Give it a stir and allow the tea to steep for about 5 minutes, until dark and smelling fragrant and spicy. Remove the aromatics, and the tea bags.

Check the dates are all pitted (so there are absolutely no stones remaining) and then drop the dates into the jug of strong tea. Leave until the tea is cool (about 10-15 minutes).

Once the tea has cooled down, lift out all except four of the dates, leaving these in the tea. The dates you've lifted out, give them a squeeze to remove excess liquid, and drop them into the food processor with the coconut. Blitz for a few seconds until smooth and then press firmly down into a small, cling-film lined container. To give you an idea of size, I use an old plastic takeaway container. Cover with cling film and leave in the fridge to set for 3-4 hours or overnight. Pop the jug with the remaining tea and the four extra dates you left in the jug with it, into the fridge also.

Once you're ready to make the topping, take the cake out of the fridge and lift out onto a serving board or plate, peeling off the cling film. You should have a solid slab.

Open the coconut cream and spread it all over the top of the cake, evenly.

To make the salted chai tea drizzle, tip away all but a couple of tablespoons of the chai tea and add a good pinch of sea salt to the now very-soaked dates. Blend this, with the dates that are still in the jug, so you end up with a caramel-like mixture. Using a spoon (or a piping bag if you like), drizzle this mixture all over the top of the cake. Cut into squares and serve.

Strawberries and Basil with Lime Coconut Cream

So we're used to eating strawberries. We know what they taste like. And basil - that's for making pesto with and scattering over a salad. But something happens when you eat the two together. It tastes nothing like strawberries and nothing like basil, but more like a tropical pineapple flavour. I love them together in this recipe, with a lime coconut cream alongside. I buy coconut cream in cartons but you can also chill a can of full fat coconut milk and then clip off the disc of cream that forms on the top. Serves 2.

100ml (1/2 cup) coconut cream
juice of 1 lime

3 large basil leaves
6 large strawberries

Method
Place the coconut cream in a bowl and squeeze over the lime juice, stirring well to mix. Divide the coconut cream between two serving bowls.

Next, chop or quarter the strawberries and add them to the bowls with the cream. Rip the basil leaves to release their aromatic oils and then scatter the leaves over the strawberries. Serve with more lime juice if you like.

Cinnamon Dusted Fried Sweet Plantains

I often use plantains in my cooking, but more often they're green plantains for making tostones or blending into muffins. This recipe came about after I had a couple of plantains on the worktop that had turned completely black. Don't throw them out - put them to good use with this sweet treat. The very ripe plantain has a toffee-like, caramel sweetness, which is boosted by the cinnamon sugar sprinkled over the top. Serves 2.

1 very ripe plantain, the skin turned completely black
1 tbsp coconut oil
2 pinches of coconut palm sugar
small pinch of cinnamon

Method
Peel your plantain to reveal the custardy yellow flesh underneath. Slice it into chunks, as you would if you were making tostones, and heat the oil in a frying pan.
Fry the plantain slices for about 3-4 minutes per side, until they look golden on both sides - and soft.

While they're cooking - keeping a watchful eye on them so they don't burn - mix the coconut sugar and cinnamon in a small bowl.

Once the plantains are cooked through and golden, transfer them, still hot, to plates and sprinkle a little of the cinnamon sugar over the top. Let them cool to just warm and then serve.

Tropical Ginger and Kale Green Smoothie

I thought my children would never drink a green smoothie, but they love this one. By looking at it, you'd expect it to taste of veggies, but it tastes like sweet, tropical fruit. It's a great way to get an extra portion of greens into your diet, without you even noticing. Makes 1.

small chunk of ginger, peeled (about the size of the tip of your finger)
small handful of fresh kale leaves, tough stalks removed, and washed well
large handful of papaya or mango, or a combination of both (I used frozen)
juice of 1 large orange
splash of filtered water

Method
Add all the ingredients to a blender and blitz until smooth. Taste, adding a little more ginger if you like. Drink straight away.

Spiced Orange Gummies

Whenever I think of winter and spices like cinnamon, cloves and ginger I always associate them with oranges. So it seemed natural that I would make a spiced orange gummies recipe - full of healing gelatin and speckled with warm spices. Makes 12-14 gummies.

juice of 2 oranges (this gave me about half a cup)
pinch of ground ginger
pinch of ground cinnamon
large pinch of ground cloves
1 tsp honey (optional)
3 tbsp flavourless gelatin

Method
Squeeze the orange juice and pour it into a small saucepan. Add the spices and stir gently. Sprinkle on the gelatin and heat the mixture very gently, stirring. Once the orange juice is warm and the gelatin has melted, pour into a small jug and then into moulds. Leave on the worktop to set at room temperature for one hour and then transfer carefully to the fridge to firm up for another hour or two. Once the gummies are set, carefully release them from their moulds and store in a lidded container in the fridge.

Roasted Blackberries with Vanilla and Matcha Tea Coconut Cream

Never roasted berries? When heated, they give off their beautiful sticky, dark juice and they seem to have a much richer flavour than when eaten raw. You can choose whether to eat these roasted berries with the Matcha coconut cream - the Matcha has quite a bitter flavour, which contrasts with the sweetness of the berries, which are flavoured with maple syrup and vanilla. I quite like this tartness. If you need to sweeten the coconut cream to counteract some of the bitterness, just beat in a little maple syrup before serving, or omit or reduce the quantity of matcha. Small quantities of Matcha are allowed on AIP, in moderation. Serves 2.

150g (5oz) fresh blackberries, washed and gently dried with a clean towel
1 tsp good vanilla extract
1 tbsp maple syrup (plus more for serving, if you like)
6 tbsp coconut cream
half a teaspoon Matcha powder

Method
First, line a shallow roasting or baking tray with greaseproof paper. Preheat your oven to gas mark 7/220°C/425°F. Arrange the blackberries in one layer in the tray, and drizzle over the vanilla extract and maple syrup. Slide into the oven for 10 minutes, until the berries are sizzling and have started to release their syrupy juices.

While the berries are roasting, quickly mix the coconut cream and the Matcha powder together. Taste and then add a small drizzle of maple syrup if you like it a bit sweeter.

Serve the berries with the Matcha coconut cream.

Carrot Cake Pancakes

A warmly-spiced carrot cake was always my favourite choice whenever there was cake on offer. The cinnamon and cloves providing some spice against the sweetness of the carrots, which you wouldn't even know were there if it weren't for the tiny flecks of orange in the cake. It was during a frosty morning, when I was craving carrot cake and discovered a black, ripe plantain in the fridge, that I set to work and created this recipe. It has the overall flavour of carrot cake, and satisfies a craving pretty well. For best results mash the plantain really well with a fork, for a smoother, sweeter pancake. You could tumble some raisins into the mixture too, if you like. Serves 2-3 (makes 5 pancakes).

1 ripe, black plantain
quarter teaspoon ground cloves
half a teaspoon ground cinnamon
half teaspoon vanilla extract
small pinch of salt
a small 8cm long piece of carrot, or a very small carrot, peeled and trimmed
1 tbsp mild, unflavoured coconut oil
maple syrup, to serve

Method
Peel and roughly chop the plantain and place in a bowl. Add the cloves, cinnamon, vanilla and salt, and mash with a fork until you have a smooth batter. Finely grate the carrot and stir it into the mixture.

Heat the coconut oil in a large pan and add heaped tablespoons of the batter, smoothing it out into a pancake-shape as you go. Keep the heat fairly low so the pancakes don't burn. Fry for about 1-2 minutes and then flip them over. Once cooked through and slightly golden in colour, serve with maple syrup.

Orange, Pineapple and Mint Drink

We often think of mint as a good herb to flavour drinks, but it wasn't until I tried pineapple with mint that I found it worked so well. Mixing fresh orange juice, pineapple chunks and then infusing with mint gives you a clean, fresh, tropical flavour. It's one of our favourites. Serves 1.

70g (2.5 oz) fresh pineapple chunks, chilled if possible

juice of 1 large orange
chilled water
3 fresh mint leaves

Method
Add the pineapple chunks and orange juice to a blender and blitz until smooth. Pour into a glass and top up with fresh, chilled water. Drop in the mint leaves and push them down with a spoon, bruising the leaves to help release its sweet aromas. Drink cold.

Blueberry, Lemon and Thyme Fizz

I tried blueberries with a range of different herbs and found that thyme was one of the best combinations. There's a floral fragrance to the tiny, dark green leaves that contrasts against the sharp sweetness of the berries. Here I've combined them in a fizzy drink, beautiful sipped on a summer's day. Makes 2-3 drinks.

Handful blueberries (I used frozen)
the juice of 1 lemon
sparkling water
4-5 sprigs of fresh thyme

Method
Add the blueberries to a blender jug and add the lemon juice. Blitz until a smooth, dark ice cream-like paste is formed. Scrape out a dessertspoonful and place in each glass. Top up with fizzy water and stir. Push a couple of thyme sprigs into each drink and finish with a lemon slice, if you like.

Strawberry and Lemon Fizz with Basil

I love how this two-tone drink plays with the senses. It's sweet and fruity, with a sharp tartness to it, thanks to the lemon. The basil rounds off all the sweetness and is a perfect partner for the strawberries. I love this drink served in retro champagne glasses - it feels like a really special treat. Roll on summer! Makes 2.

200g fresh strawberries, hulled
juice of 1 lemon
splash of chilled water
3-4 fresh basil leaves
sparkling water, to top up

Method
Tumble the strawberries into a blender and squeeze in the lemon juice. Add a splash of water (about half an espresso cup's worth) and blitz. Divide the mixture between two glasses and drop a couple of fresh basil leaves in each. Top up with sparkling water. You'll get a two-tone drink with the ruby-red strawberry drink below and the cloud of strawberry basil fizz on top. Muddle the basil by pushing it down into the drink to release more of its aromatic oils. Beautiful.

Bacon Maple Cinnamon Pancakes
These plantain based pancakes combine salty, smoky bacon with the sweet warmth of ground cinnamon and vanilla. Perfect for an indulgent breakfast. Makes 8 pancakes, serves 3-4.

1 large, ripe (totally black) plantain
quarter teaspoon cinnamon
half teaspoon vanilla extract
1 tbsp cooking fat (use mild, unflavoured coconut oil or lard)
4-6 slices of smoked, streaky bacon, grilled or fried in a dry pan until crisp
small drizzle of maple syrup, to serve

Method

First, peel the plantain and mash the pale yellow, custard-coloured flesh with a fork. Stir in the cinnamon and vanilla and mix until well combined.

Heat a little oil or fat in a large frying pan and drop in tablespoonfuls of the plantain mixture, letting them sizzle. Using a spatula, tease and spread the drops into thin circles. Keep them on a low heat, making sure they don't burn. Once the underside is golden, carefully flip them over and continue to cook on the other side.

Once the pancakes are cooked (you might need to cook them in batches, depending on the size of your pan), pile them up on a serving plate with folded slices of the cooked bacon inbetween and drizzle with a little maple syrup.

Sauces and Finishing Touches

Here, I've included recipes for sauces and seasonings that you can serve alongside your favourite dishes. I've also included the basic versions of some of the curry pastes in the book, to give you a handy, quick reference guide.

Here, you'll find basic curry pastes to use in your soups, curries and stews - and marinades that you can use with your favourite seafood, meats and fish. There are also salad dressings and a range of flavoured salts to finish off your food with a bang. Some have unusual flavour combinations, so have fun trying them out and adapting them with any other ingredients that come to mind as you cook.

Basic AIP Green Thai Curry Paste

If you're after a basic green Thai curry paste that's still tasty even though there are no nightshades in it, then look no further. You can add spoonfuls of this paste to burger mixtures or soups, stews or curries. Fry off the paste before adding your coconut milk, for a tasty Thai-style curry or soup.

2 sticks of lemongrass, sliced
2 cloves of garlic, peeled and roughly chopped
big handful fresh coriander leaf/cilantro
handful fresh basil leaves (you can use Thai Basil if you can find it, instead, if you like)
juice of half a lime
1 cm thick slice of ginger, peeled
2 spring onions, trimmed
half a teaspoon of fish sauce (optional)

Method
Place all the ingredients in a blender or food processor and blitz well until smooth. Use straight away in your recipe or scrape into a suitable container and store in the fridge for up to 2 days.

Basic AIP Red Thai Curry Paste

This is the basic paste that I used in my Red Thai Vegetable Curry. You can make a batch of this paste and use it to add to burger or meatball mixtures or as the basis for a coconut milk based soup. It has a sweet, Red Thai inspired flavour, but without the heat as there are no chillies in it. If you want a bit more spice, either up the quantity of ginger or grate in some fresh horseradish root, if you like.

2 sticks of lemongrass
2 cloves of garlic
bunch of fresh coriander leaf/cilantro
bunch of fresh basil leaves
juice of half a lime
1 tsp worth of freshly grated or chopped ginger
a few drops (about quarter of a teaspoon) fish sauce
1 small cooked beetroot

Method
Blitz everything in a food processor until it forms a coarse paste. Either use straight away in your favourite recipes or scrape into a lidded container and store in the fridge. Keeps for up to 2 days.

Basic AIP Indian Style Marinade

For a basic Indian style marinade, like the one I use for my Indian style whole roast chicken or chicken wings, try this. Mix it all up together and slather over fish, seafood or meats before grilling or frying. Best made just before using, otherwise store in the fridge for up to 2 days.

1 clove garlic, peeled and grated
1 tsp ginger, grated
1 heaped teaspoon ground turmeric
2 tbsp coconut yoghurt
zest and juice from 1 lemon
good pinch of salt
half teaspoon dried coriander leaf/cilantro
small pinch of ground cloves

Method
In a bowl, stir all the ingredients together and use to marinate your favourite seafood, fish or meats. Use straight away, or it will keep for 2-3 days covered in a suitable container, in the fridge.

Bacon Jam

This sweet-smoky, sticky jam is perfect for serving with burgers or grilled or roasted meats. It makes quite a lot - freeze half if you think you won't use it straight away. Many conventional recipes for bacon jam include coffee, refined sugars and nightshades such as tomatoes. This is totally AIP-compliant. Makes about 20 servings - keep in the fridge for about a week or freeze half for later.

500g (1lb) smoked, streaky bacon, chopped into small pieces (the smaller, the better)
3 cloves garlic, peeled and roughly chopped
1 red onion, peeled and finely chopped
3 x 15ml tablespoons maple syrup
2 x teaspoons apple cider vinegar
250ml (1 cup) rich beef broth

1 tsp vanilla extract
5-6 tablespoons no-mato sauce

Method
Finely chop up your bacon and gently fry, to release the fats, in a medium to large-sized saucepan, stirring regularly. If your bacon isn't very fatty, you can add a little coconut oil or duck fat to help it along, but not too much.

Once most of the fat has rendered down from the bacon add the chopped onion and garlic cloves. Stir-fry for a couple of minutes until the onion has started to soften and the bacon is golden. Add the maple syrup, cider vinegar, beef broth and vanilla extract and stir, bringing to a gentle simmer. Cook on a low heat for another 20 minutes or so, until most of the liquid has evaporated but you still have a small amount in the bottom of the pan. Stir in the no-mato sauce until it's warmed through and then turn off the heat and allow to cool.

If you want it more thinner and jammier, you can chop the bacon up a bit more in a processor, but I like it quite chunky.

Once cool, store in an airtight container in the fridge, or freeze it in portion sizes. If refrigerated, use within a week.

Comfort Bites NoMato Sauce

This nightshade-free version of tomato sauce is handy to have up your sleeve. I make a big batch and then freeze some in individual portions for later, to save me the work of making again the next time. Add your own herbs and spices as you wish, and you'll be making AIP-compliant Italian style stews in no time. Makes a perfect sauce for AIP-compliant pizzas, meatballs or serving with fish or chicken. You can also add a spoonful to your curries for a more tomato-like texture and flavour. Makes enough for 8 servings.

half tsp cooking fat (coconut or avocado oil, bacon fat or lard)
6 medium-sized carrots, trimmed, peeled and chopped
3 medium-sized cooked (and peeled) beetroot, chopped
1 large onion, peeled and chopped
4 small celery sticks, chopped
3 cloves garlic, chopped
2 splashes (about 150ml) red wine
half teaspoon dried thyme
500ml (2 cups) good beef stock, or broth
pinch of salt

Method
Heat the fat or oil in a medium-sized saucepan and add the chopped vegetables. Let everything cook for 4-5 minutes and then add the wine and thyme. Let the alcohol simmer off and then pour in the beef stock. Add a good pinch of salt, put the lid on the pan and let the sauce cook until the vegetables are all soft - about 20 minutes.

Once the veggies are all tender, take off the lid and blend the sauce until smooth. Serve straight away.

AIP-Compliant Argentine Chimichurri Salsa

This is pretty close to the chimichurri I learned to make in Buenos Aires. The locals add a pinch of paprika and this is left out on the autoimmune protocol as it's a nightshade spice. So this is an AIP version. I use it in my stuffed chicken breast recipe in the book, and we have a bowl of it at every barbecue for all the grilled meats. It goes with pretty much anything. Makes about 8 spoonfuls.

8 cloves of garlic, peeled and finely chopped
medium bunch of flat-leaf parsley (about 12g) chopped (including the stalks)
4 tbsp extra virgin olive oil
2 tbsp apple cider vinegar
pinch of sea salt

Method
Either chop the parsley and garlic finely, or blitz in a processor if you prefer it smooth. Trickle in the olive oil and vinegar and season with salt, to taste. Adjust the quantities of vinegar or salt until you're happy with the flavour and then spoon into a container or jar and store in the fridge until needed. The chimichurri gets better the next day, so feel free to make it a day in advance, although it will keep for up to 2 days.

Horseradish Sauce

Horseradish sauce is a spicy, creamy accompaniment to usually beef, but it's also good with any smoked fish. Here's my AIP version.

3 heaped tbsp coconut cream
1 heaped tsp freshly finely grated horseradish root
1 tsp finely chopped fresh parsley
large pinch of salt
extra virgin oil, for topping

Method
Mix the ingredients together until smooth. Use straight away, or cover and keep in the fridge until ready to eat.

AIP Sweet and Sour Sauce

I went a long time craving a takeaway-style Chinese sweet and sour sauce. And, after quite a few tries at this recipe, this is the version I fell in love with. This recipe makes a quarter of a cupful, which isn't very much, but it's the kind of sauce you need to make as you need it, rather than store in the fridge. We found this amount was perfect for two of us to share or use as a dip. Makes a quarter of a cup - just enough for dipping.

2 tbsp apple cider vinegar
2 heaped tbsp runny honey
1 garlic clove, peeled
1cm thick slice of ginger, peeled
3cm long piece of raw carrot, grated or very finely chopped
6 tbsp beef or chicken broth or stock
1 spring onion, to garnish

Method
Put the apple cider vinegar and the honey in a small saucepan. Finely grate in the garlic clove and the ginger and then add the carrot. Pour in the stock or broth and bring everything to a gentle simmer. Once the carrot is cooked and is completely tender, blend the sauce until smooth (I do this with a stick blender in a small jug). Garnish with chopped spring onion and cool slightly before serving.

Italian Herb Pink Salt

Here's a salt blend packed full of different herbs that are often used in Italian cooking, You can add a pinch of this salt to vegetables, salad dressings, grilled pork, chicken, beef or use it to season burgers.

2 tbsp Himalayan Pink Salt
quarter tsp dried basil
half teaspoon dried rosemary
quarter teaspoon dried oregano
1 bay leaf

Method
Put all the ingredients in a spice blender or grinder and blend until the texture you like. Store in an airtight container.

Nori Salt

Nori is a really good source of minerals like iodine and calcium. Making nori salt is one easy way of upping your intake of nutrients and adding a deep, savoury flavour to your food at the same time. It's great with salmon, fish, seafood, chicken, pork and beef.

1 tbsp sea salt flakes
small strip (about half a sheet) of nori

Method
Put the sea salt flakes in a spice grinder or small processor and rip up the nori into small paper-like pieces. Drop them in with the salt and blend until combined. Store in an airtight container.

Saffron and Rosemary Salt

Saffron is a fragrant spice used in many places all over the world. In this flavoured salt it is mixed with rosemary. This salt is good for rubbing over fish or seafood before grilling, or over poultry or pork.

1 tbsp sea salt crystals or flakes
half teaspoon of rosemary
good pinch of saffron threads

Method
In a spice grinder or processor, blend all the ingredients until at the consistency you like. Store in an airtight container.

Porcini and Thyme Salt

This flavoured salt is used in the Crispy-Skinned Chicken Breast with Porcini and Thyme Salt Crust recipe in the Mains section. It contains dried porcini mushrooms and gives dishes a heady, woody scent. The thyme lifts the flavour and adds fragrance. This salt is also great with pork - I like to sprinkle a good pinch of it over pork before roasting.

1 tsp sea salt crystals or flakes
quarter tsp dried thyme
2-3 dried porcini mushrooms

Method
In a spice grinder or processor mix together the ingredients until they're at the consistency you're after - I personally like some texture in the salt crystals and don't blend them too smooth. Store in an airtight container.

Peppery Green Goddess Dressing with Watercress

Watercress is high in vitamin C and so when you blend it into a salad dressing you're getting a whole extra level of nutrients as a bonus. I love this creamy dressing with salmon or chicken. It would also work well with tuna, too. Makes 1 small jar.

2 tbsp extra virgin olive oil
1 small avocado, peeled and the pit removed
large handful of fresh watercress
1 tbsp apple cider vinegar
pinch of salt

Method
Place all the ingredients in a blender and blitz until smooth. Store in the fridge and eat up within 3 days.

Instant Rosemary Oil

You can make infused oils, but they sometimes need a day or more for the flavours to settle. Here's a really quick rosemary-scented oil that you can whip up as you need it. Drizzle over cooked vegetables, roasted lamb or salads. Makes about 3 tbsp - enough for a salad dressing or drizzle - make more if you need to.

3 tbsp extra virgin olive oil
a sprig of fresh rosemary

Method
Trickle the oil into a small container like a cup, mug or ramekin. Add the sprig of rosemary and bash and mash it gently using the handle of a spoon, to bruise the leaves and release some of their flavour into the oil. Use straight away on your favourite recipe.

Chip Shop Style Curry Sauce

One of the sides I always used to pick up from the chip shop was a polystyrene cup of mild curry sauce that I'd always dip my chips into. And it was one of the things I missed once I started the autoimmune protocol. This nightshade and seed-free version tastes quite like the real thing and takes just minutes to make. You just heat the ingredients in a saucepan and then blend it up using a stick blender. Use it to serve alongside anything you like - burgers, sausages, grilled meats or veggies. I love to dip parsnip fries into it. This is the taste of my childhood. Makes enough for 2 servings.

1 small onion, peeled and chopped
1 apple from the fruit bowl
1 clove garlic, peeled and chopped
pinch of ground cloves
half a teaspoon turmeric powder
200ml (about three quarters of a cup) chicken stock
pinch of salt, to taste

Method
Place the chopped onion in a small saucepan. Quickly peel the apple and core it (discard the peel and core) and chop it up, adding it to the pan with the onion. Add the cloves, turmeric and garlic and pour in the chicken stock. Bring to a gentle simmer and cook, stirring, until the apple and onion
are both tender and the stock is hot. Once everything's hot and cooked, turn off the heat and blend until smooth.

Taste, adding a pinch of salt if you think it needs it. Serve warm, with your choice of veggie fries.

Indian-Style Mint Dip

I always remembered the mint dips that were served alongside poppadoms or onion bhajis. This is my version. It's very simple to make, and has a less sweet, more minty flavour that works well drizzled over onion bhajis, Indian chicken or lamb burgers. Serves 2-3.

200ml (three-quarters of a cup) full-fat coconut milk
a bunch of fresh mint (about 28g)
pinch of salt
1 garlic clove, peeled

Method
Pour the coconut milk into a blender jug. Pick the leaves off the bunch of fresh mint and add them to the jug, along with the pinch of salt and the peeled garlic clove. Blend until smooth, into a speckled, green dip. Serve straight away.

Roasted Garlic

Garlic has a pungent, strong flavour - unless it's been roasted. Roasting garlic gives you golden, sweet, caramelised cloves that are soft and spreadable. Whizz roasted garlic into salad dressings, sauces or serve as it is alongside roasted meats. I'll quite often tuck in a foil-wrapped bulb of garlic next to a joint of meat if I'm roasting it in the oven, so we can eat the cloves alongside. If you're cooking a joint of meat in the slow cooker, as in the Thyme and Sea Salt Pulled Pork, you can also tuck a bulb of garlic in the slow cooker along with it if you like. Makes 1 bulb/head of garlic.

Method
Just take the whole bulb of garlic and place sideways on a chopping board. With a sharp knife, just cut off the very top of the pointy end of the bulb, away from the root, so you reveal the very tips of the cloves inside. Cut off a square of foil and place the bulb on top of it, drizzling with a little olive or avocado oil. Loosely wrap up the garlic and roast, on a baking tray for 45 minutes, at about 200°C/400°F/gas mark 6. Take it out of the oven (it'll be hot) and allow it to cool slightly on a board or plate on the kitchen worktop. Once slightly cooled, tip the bulb upside down and squeeze the cloves out from their papery skins.

Basil Oil

I love basil oil for two main reasons. Firstly, it's a low-FODMAP substitute for pesto, because it doesn't contain any garlic but you still get all the sweet flavour of the basil to spoon over your chicken, fish or zoodles. And secondly, it's so easy to make - you just make up a jar at a time, keep it in the fridge and spoon it over whatever you want to eat. It's great with grilled and roasted chicken and pretty much all vegetables. I use it in my grilled courgette recipe in the Sides *section of the book. Thin it out a little bit with extra oil if you want a looser texture. This basil oil is intended as a drizzle to go over foods rather than as a marinade to be cooked in, so spoon it over fish, chicken, lamb, beef, veg... pretty much anything you like. Store in a lidded container in the fridge and use within 3 days. Makes just over half a cup.*

1 bunch of basil
half a cup extra virgin olive oil

Method
Wash and dry the basil leaves and place them in the bottom of a blender jug. Pour in the olive oil and put on the lid. Blend until a smooth paste is formed, trickling in a little more oil for a looser texture.

Acknowledgements

This book has been so much fun for me to produce and I've learned so much along the way. I never look at a sprig of thyme or a papery bulb of garlic in the same way.

It's my aim that the recipes in this book will help inspire people to play around with spices and herbs a bit more in their cooking and enjoy pairing them up with other ingredients and find new, exciting combinations. Go for it!

I am so grateful for all of you, who read the blog and support me on social media channels like Facebook, Instagram and Twitter. Your comments, likes and shares inspire me to continue to create healthy, tasty recipes for you all. I love your feedback and seeing your photos of my recipes you've made. You are all part of this huge conversation around food, diet and health and we are all moving in a positive direction and helping and inspiring others to adopt a healthier, more veggie-rich way of life. And it's amazing. It makes me so excited every day to log on and talk to you all. So thank you. You all made this book possible.

When I first started blogging about AIP and moving in a healthier direction with the blog, it all felt so lonely. There were only a handful of bloggers sharing recipes. But now, I am so proud to be part of a huge online AIP community and many of these bloggers and writers I now count as my friends. I am inspired by your battles with your health as well as your beautiful recipes and advice. Thank you all.

My husband really has put up with me through everything. Thanks Jav for your constant support and encouragement, and being as excited as I was to create this book.

My children are my recipe testers. And they're very honest. If they love a recipe, they'll tell me. If not, they'll definitely tell me. Thanks Georgina and Sofia for not complaining at the dinner table. It was all worth it. And I still managed to get you to eat your veggies.

References and Further Reading

S. Ballantyne. (July 26, 2012) Spices On The Autoimmune Protocol. In *The Paleo Mom*. Retrieved from: http://www.thepaleomom.com/2012/07/spices-on-autoimmune-protocol.html

Nice, Jill. *Herbal Remedies For Healing* (1998 edition) Judy Piatkus Publishers, London.

Natural News, Parsley is an Effective Antioxidant, Diuretic, Blood Tonic and More. Retrieved from: http://www.naturalnews.com/035044_parsley_antioxidants_blood.html

The American Academy of Neurological and Orthopaedic Surgeons. Human Male Sexual Response to Olfactory Stimuli. Retrieved from: http://aanos.org/human-male-sexual-response-to-olfactory-stimuli/

Berriedale-Johnson, Michelle. Food Fit For Pharoahs (1999) The British Museum Press.

The list of spices in the first chapter are adapted from the following two resources, which I used as a reference point and then added more spices and herbs in from my own research. The *Spices On The Autoimmune Protocol* blog post by The Paleo Mom: http://www.thepaleomom.com/2012/07/spices-on-autoimmune-protocol.html and *Spices on the AIP* by Phoenix Helix: http://www.phoenixhelix.com/2014/11/02/spices-on-the-aip/

Further Reading

If you want to find out more about the autoimmune protocol do have a look at the book The Paleo Approach by Sarah Ballantyne, which goes into the science behind autoimmunity as well as the basis for the AIP diet. I'm proud to be listed as a Paleo Approach Approved blogger - for a full list of other bloggers who write about Sarah Ballantyne's AIP, visit the link above for more inspiration.

Index of Recipes

What Do You Fancy?

Indian Inspired

Thai Inspired

Chinese Inspired

AIP Chinese Style Beef Noodle Soup, 34
Honey Ginger Stir-Fried Beef with Cabbage, 49
Chinese Style Sweet and Sour Tamarind Prawns, 53
AIP Chinese-Style Lemon Chicken, 66
Chinese Takeout Inspired Seaweed, 84
AIP Sweet and Sour Sauce, 117

***

Dietary Requirements

Vegan and Vegetarian (no dairy in AIP)

Garlic Plantain Chips with Zesty Guacamole, 30
Mushroom and Fennel Soup (use vegetable stock in place of the chicken stock), 31
Spicy Broccoli and Ginger Soup (use vegetable stock), 32
Creamy Carrot and Lemongrass Soup (use vegetable stock), 35
Spring Greens Soup with Basil Oil (use vegetable stock), 37
Indian Style Sweet Potato Patties, 37
AIP Onion Bhajis, 38
Sweet Potato, Spring Onion and Ginger Soup (use vegetable stock), 40
Naan Bread Asian Pizza (top with more vegetables in place of the chicken), 54
AIP Red Thai Vegetable Curry (skip the fish sauce), 71
Coriander and Garlic Naan Breads, 77
Roasted Squash with Rosemary and Honey (vegetarian), 78
Raw Carrot Salad with Ginger and Lime Dressing, 79
Quick Balsamic Caramelised Onions, 81
Salted Plantain Fries with Garlic and Parsley, 82
Beetroot Salad with Garlic and Parsley, 85
Artichoke Salad with Chives and Garlic, 86

Coconut Free

The following recipes are coconut free, except for the coconut oil used to cook them. Just use a different cooking oil like lard, bacon fat or avocado oil where coconut oil is mentioned.

Roasted Garlic, 122
Basil Oil, 123

Low FODMAP

I've checked the ingredients for these recipes against low-FODMAP food lists, but please double check that they are suitable for you personally, as there can be variations in different low-FODMAP lists and tolerances can vary.

AIP Ginger and Salmon Sushi Maki Rolls, 33
Tuna, Palm Heart and Coriander Salad, 40
Rib-eye Steak with Horseradish Sauce Dip, 57
Slow Cooked Lamb Shanks with Paleo Mint Sauce (omit
    the honey), 60
Slow Cooker Thyme and Sea Salt Pulled Pork Shoulder, 62
Pheasant Saltimbocca, 63
Scallops with Saffron and Orange, 74
Raw Carrot Salad with Ginger and Lime Dressing, 79
Spaghetti Squash with Bacon and Crispy Sage, 83
Grilled Courgettes with Basil Oil, 93
Mint Mojito, 95
Pomegranate Fizz, 96
Warm Chai Tea, 97
Strawberries and Basil with Lime Coconut Cream, 102
Spiced Orange Gummies, 104
Blueberry, Lemon and Thyme Fizz, 108
Strawberry and Lemon Fizz with Basil, 108
Horseradish Sauce, 116
Italian Herb Pink Salt, 118
Nori Salt, 118
Saffron and Rosemary Salt, 119
Instant Rosemary Oil, 120
Basil Oil, 123

Index of Ingredients

Parsnip Saag Aloo, 89
Indian Style Mushroom Cauliflower
Rice, 92
Raw Chai Tea Cake with Salted Caramel
Chai Tea Frosting, 100
Tropical Ginger and Kale Green
Smoothie, 104
Spiced Orange Gummies, 104
Basic AIP Green Thai Curry Paste, 111
Basic AIP Red Thai Curry Paste, 112
Basic AIP Indian Style Marinade, 112
AIP Sweet and Sour Sauce, 117

H

Himalayan Pink Sea Salt
Italian Herb Pink Salt, 118

Honey
Honey Ginger Stir-Fried Beef with
Cabbage, 49
Chinese Style Sweet and Sour Tamarind
Prawns, 53
Slow Cooked Lamb Shanks with Paleo
Mint Sauce, 60
AIP Chinese-Style Lemon Chicken, 66
Smoky, Sweet, Herby Pork Ribs, 75
Roasted Squash with Rosemary and
Honey, 78
Honey Swirl Cinnamon Ice Cream, 97
Spiced Orange Gummies, 104
AIP Sweet and Sour Sauce, 117

Horseradish Root
Rib-eye Steak with Horseradish Sauce
Dip, 57
Spicy Horseradish Beets with Smoked
Mackerel, 61
Horseradish Sauce, 116

I, J

K

Kale
Chinese Takeout-Style Seaweed, 84
Tropical Ginger and Kale Green
Smoothie, 104

King Prawns
Roasted King Prawns with Smoked
Garlic, Coriander and Lime, 44

L

Lamb
Lamb and Saffron Stew, 48
Egyptian Lamb Artichoke Hash, 52
Lamb and Mint Meatball, Red Onion and
Sweet Potato Bake, 58
Slow Cooked Lamb Shanks with Paleo
Mint Sauce, 60
Lamb Do Piaza, 68

Leek
Spring Greens Soup with Basil Oil, 37

Lemon
AIP Onion Bhajis, 38
Indian Style Whole Roast Chicken, 50
Egyptian Lamb Artichoke Hash, 52
Lemon and Dill Smoked Mackerel
Salad, 65
AIP Chinese-Style Lemon Chicken, 66
Roasted Salmon and Parsnips with Dill
Gremolata, 73
Grilled Courgettes with Basil Oil, 93
Blueberry, Lemon and Thyme Fizz, 108
Strawberry and Lemon Fizz with
Basil, 108
Basic AIP Indian Style Marinade, 112

Lemongrass
Fragrant Herb and Coconut Chicken
Soup, 28
Creamy Carrot and Lemongrass Soup, 35
Thai Inspired Turkey Meatball Curry, 42
AIP Red Thai Vegetable Curry, 71
Basic AIP Green Thai Curry Paste, 111
Basic AIP Red Thai Curry Paste, 112

Lettuce
Tuna, Palm Heart and Coriander Salad, 40

Lime
Fragrant Herb and Coconut Chicken
Soup, 28
Garlic Plantain Chips with Zesty
Guacamole, 30

Sherry Vinegar
Beetroot Salad with Garlic and Parsley, 85

Sparkling Water
Mint Mojito, 95
Pomegranate Fizz, 96
Blueberry, Lemon and Thyme Fizz, 108
Strawberry and Lemon Fizz with
Basil, 108

Spinach
Mutton and Spinach Curry, 47
Rib-eye Steak with Horseradish Sauce
Dip, 57
Lemon and Dill Smoked Mackerel
Salad, 65
Creamy Spinach and Chicken Curry, 70
Parsnip Saag Aloo, 89

Spring Greens
Spring Greens Soup with Basil Oil, 37

Squash
Roasted Squash with Rosemary and
Honey, 78

Squash, Spaghetti
Spaghetti Squash with Bacon and Crispy
Sage, 83

Strawberries
Strawberries and Basil with Lime Coconut
Cream, 102
Strawberry and Lemon Fizz with
Basil, 108

Sweet Potato
Indian Style Sweet Potato Patties, 37
Sweet Potato, Spring Onion and Ginger
Soup, 40
Indian-Style Turkey Breakfast Hash, 56
Lamb and Mint Meatball, Red Onion and
Sweet Potato Bake, 58
Sweet Potato and Chive Mash, 80
BBQ Sweet Potato Fries, 87
Bacon and Rosemary Hasselback Sweet
Potatoes, 88
Roasted Sweet Potato and Red Onion with
Black Garlic, 90

T

Tamarind Paste
Chinese Style Sweet and Sour Tamarind
Prawns, 53

Tapioca Flour
AIP Onion Bhajis, 38
AIP Chinese-Style Lemon Chicken, 66

Tea, black
Warm Chai Tea, 97
Chai Tea Ice Lollies, 99
Raw Chai Tea Cake with Salted Caramel
Chai Tea Frosting, 100

Thyme
Slow Cooker Thyme and Sea Salt Pulled
Pork Shoulder, 62
Smoky, Sweet, Herby Pork Ribs, 75
BBQ Sweet Potato Fries, 87
Roasted Balsamic Mushrooms with
Thyme, 87
Blueberry, Lemon and Thyme Fizz, 108
Comfort Bites NoMato Sauce, 114
Porcini and Thyme Salt, 119

Tuna
Tuna, Palm Heart and Coriander Salad, 40

Turkey
Thai Inspired Turkey Meatball Curry, 42
Indian-Style Turkey Breakfast Hash, 56

Turmeric
Indian-Style Sweet Potato Patties, 37
AIP Onion Bhajis, 38
Thai Inspired Turkey Meatball Curry, 42
Mutton and Spinach Curry, 47
Indian Style Whole Roast Chicken, 50
Egyptian Lamb Artichoke Hash, 52
Indian-Style Turkey Breakfast Hash, 56
Lamb Do Piaza, 68
Creamy Spinach and Chicken Curry, 70
AIP Red Thai Vegetable Curry, 71
Parsnip Saag Aloo, 89
Indian Style Mushroom Cauliflower
Rice, 92
Basic AIP Indian Style Marinade, 112
Chip Shop Style Curry Sauce, 121

Jo Romero lives in the UK and is the author of www.comfortbites.co.uk - the food blog that's dedicated to showing that good, healthy, comforting food can be enjoyed by everyone, no matter what their diet and lifestyle. She is also the author of AIP Cookbooks *Simple AIP Comfort Food* and *AIP Snacks and Quick Lunches,* both available on Amazon. Keep up to date with her on Instagram and Twitter @joromerofood. Enjoyed this book? Then please do consider leaving feedback on Amazon, so others can find it, too. Thank you.

***

Printed by Amazon Italia Logistica S.r.l.
Torrazza Piemonte (TO), Italy

10841766R00083